THE LAYERED HOME

THE LAYERED HOME

Inspiration for Creating Cozy, Collected Rooms

BENJAMIN REYNAERT

with Christina Poletto

Photographs by Manuel Rodriguez

MITCHELL BEAZLEY

CONTENTS

FOR THE LOVE OF LAYERS *11*

15
AN EXUBERANT EYE

65
PERSONAL MATTERS

124
CREATIVE LIVING

181
ARTFUL ARRANGEMENTS

230
AT EASE

MANY THANKS *296*

MORE THANKS... *298*

INDEX *300*

FOR THE LOVE OF LAYERS

I have always been fascinated by the truly infinite possibilities that can birth a space into existence, and especially by particular interpretations enacted by curious and creative minds. To me, the unsung heroes are those who throw away any suggested playbooks about how rooms should behave and personalize these spaces according to what *feels* right. Sometimes, that means flashy colors or offbeat patterns will properly support the vision. Other times, it might be a spasm of art in historic frames, pre-loved furniture that was scooped up at the right place and time, or a mob of imperfectly perfect ceramic figurines that occupy prime real estate on a tabletop.

As a young boy, I sometimes found myself frozen with wonder when I entered certain rooms, particularly those displaying echelons of detail both high and low (the more surfaces the better). At the time, I didn't know what this reverence meant, but I knew it was important. Almost sacred. As my career evolved, it dawned on me—the layered look is its own visual language, and one that invites an incredibly deep degree of comfort and individuality. Sure, design playbooks can be handy, especially for essential and practical purposes, but seeing how others combine pattern, form, texture, color, and personality is best learned through observation.

The intention of this book is to share favorite layered looks that have invited lots of questions and also more wonder.

The spaces featured in the pages that follow are beautifully composed and, most important, exhibit powerfully personal stories. Other similitudes inside of these homes include: a devotion to collections; sometimes many, assorted artifacts from time and travels; and zealous attention to tiny details that contribute to the collective character of a space.

In an age when trends pick up, take off, and die on social media in the span of a season, I believe in the idea of slowing down. These personal spaces are examples of dressing a room leisurely, with intention, and are ever mindful of the personality of a space, even if it's unfinished. Indeed, I am perfectly fine with a room not being done for months or years if it means holding out for the right thing that will encourage unity, not confusion. Blank spaces are just opportunities for a surface to breathe, or simply to keep room for what's meant to be there.

The places we call home, like our lives, contain multitudes. To this end, I often think about the Albert Hadley pointer that "A room should feel collected, not decorated." If you choose one playbook rule, let this be your guide: Layers plus personalization is the combination that creates absolute spatial magic. Nothing else comes close. Do these collections and layers remain changeless? Absolutely not. In fact, the beauty of the layered home is that there's a flexible impermanence to what enters, and exits, the arrangement. Knowing when to let go of things is just as important to preserving the special cohesion of a space.

From this band of experts and creatives who have welcomed me into their homes and lives, I have learned so much about the psychology and applications of collecting, arranging objects, and modifying rooms over time, and I know you will, too.

The door to the layered home is always open. Welcome!

AN *EXUBERANT* EYE

LIVE WITH THINGS YOU LOVE

Having spent over a decade getting to peek inside the homes of the designers, artists, and tastemakers I most admire, I've learned that the most successful, memorable projects incorporate things that are very much adored. Love for objects doesn't discriminate between an expensive antique with historical provenance and a whimsical souvenir from a trip or a lovely shell picked up at the beach. Knowing the difference between what's beautiful, purposeful, and meaningful and what's simply transactional is no easy task. Every detail counts, from what type of waste bin sits beneath your desk to the pen you write with. I believe in finding and using aesthetically pleasing things for even the most utilitarian of jobs. It's common in the design community to encourage someone to live with things they love. In practice, attuning oneself to this idea requires a certain self-determination and awareness of what will make a room special and meaningful to you. This often comes down to a lot of trial and error.

I myself have fallen prey to quick fixes, impulse sojourns to retail stores, and the allure of two-day shipping online when it comes to finding things for my home. These panicked purchases almost always make their way to Goodwill eventually. I've come to appreciate the long game when it comes to sourcing, actually leaving the space above a demilune table empty for a while until I find the right thing, whether that be an antique Louis Philippe mirror with a certain aged patina or the perfect piece of art to balance out the color palette of the room. One tip I've also gleaned from the pros is to keep a list of items I need, along with the desired dimensions, on my phone, because you just never know when you'll find the thing that completes a look.

The success of finding something just right for our home is often half the reason why we love those things, whether they are perceived as high-end or low-end. This tends to create a calming sense that everything is right, if not in the world, at the very least, in that corner of our room, for a small moment in time.

Butter painted the mirror black and added a radiator cover to create a usable—albeit narrow—surface for ornamental bowls, candles, and flowers. "It is a hugely useful multipurpose feature. My dear, very talented mother-in-law painted the top to look like marble. We also painted the radiator black so it disappears behind the trellis front, quite a well-known but clever trick."

at home with
BUTTER WAKEFIELD
SHEPHERD'S BUSH, LONDON

COLOR CONFIDENCE

Butter Wakefield's place is a repository for personality, layers, and quirky details. There's a wonderful sense of green throughout, which seems to pop up everywhere. Flowers that she pulls regularly from the garden are wild and have a looseness to them. While her home is a terraced townhouse in the heart of London, when one is in the front and rear outdoor spaces, you feel as if you are in the countryside.

Inside, the living areas combine big ideas like displaying many types of collections with less fussy easy-to-do concepts like pinning ribbon to a lampshade for a trickle of color. Butter is not afraid of layering a floral-patterned pillow, cushion, or blanket onto a striped piece of upholstery. Somehow, when she gathers twenty-seven patterns and colors in a space, it almost creates a more calming effect than having one or two patterns that command all the attention.

Butter's kitchen walls are covered in frames, objects, flowers, and other ephemera, creating a very personalized motif with the effect of a living wallpaper. Everything is well placed and considered, but nothing feels precious. It's very English to forgo the "kitchen island" for a dining table that serves a dual purpose: prep station (whether for food or florals) and a place for easy gatherings. The leafy-green-plant-patterned wallpaper in the hallway, quite fitting, runs up a couple flights of stairs, and beautifully appointed bedrooms and baths and a creative office radiate from it. Every room unfolds into another, each completely different from the next.

OPPOSITE: Butter's front door is painted in Hopper by Little Greene. "I adore the color green, so I thought the front door was the best place to start."

"Green has always been my favorite color," says Butter about the vivaciously verdant tint found everywhere from the entrance gate to the front door, hallway, primary bathroom, and endless places in between. Although she's quick to add: "Maybe someday I'll switch to yellow."

For now, green is going nowhere fast for the gardening designer who served formative career stints with Christie's in New York City and English textile brand Colefax and Fowler, where she gleaned art appreciation and interior design canon over the years. But in the end, it was plants that pulled her in. "I come from a long line of gardeners. My grandfather had very beautiful English gardens outside of Philadelphia. My ma's a really good gardener, and so is my aunt . . . I think it's a little osmosis and just proximity."

Osmosis seems to apply to Butter's own home, too. After all, a devotion to many versions of her beloved green is inspired by nature, but so is everything else. "I choose colors outside that I know I want to bring inside, so they definitely overlap and correlate, and complement each other," she says. "I have a lot of oranges, zinnias, geums, and orange tulips. So the year is full of colors that I feel very happy to see both inside and out." Butter says gardening delivers that happiness, too. "Everyone knows how good being outside in nature is for you and your mental health. So that plays into it, too. I feel like a garden should not only be very rich in both planting color and design but should also provide for me and for wildlife as well."

There's no hard-and-fast rule for how Butter, who got her signature nickname from her father, outfits her living spaces. "It's important to have some old things as well as some new things, some important pieces (to the extent that you can afford them) as well as some less interesting, more run-of-the-mill items." In her home, patterns appear in spades, quirky color pairings encourage a second

"The container is just as important— possibly even more so— than what goes in it."

Using the yard's rectangular space as a guide, Butter created broad side borders, 1.4 meters (about 4½ feet) deep, which affords room for ample plants. Later, she added the wildflower meadow to the mix.

look, and different shapes and textures inhabit the same spaces, looking sweetly simpatico together. And even the tiniest bits of real estate provide opportunities to show off a charming figurine, an exciting cut of ribbon, or a leafy floral. "I don't ever go out in search of that perfect thing, though I'm always on the hunt for things to put flowers in, in a variety of sizes. The container is just as important—possibly even more so—than what goes in it!"

The backyard's rectangular shape encouraged the garden's layout with generous borders and deep layers of untethered and colorful wildflowers. To commence a post-workweek recess, Butter adheres to a gentle ritual of returning to the outdoors. "The thing I like best is going into the garden and picking flowers for the weekend."

OPPOSITE: The vibrant and shiny orange inside the bookshelves is Charlotte's Locks by Farrow & Ball. The bronze library lights are Preston swing arm wall lights by Vaughan Designs, and the pleated cream and orange paper shades are by Rosi de Ruig. "I think they add a little uplift in pattern and color, which I enjoy," says Butter. The artichoke lamps are by Pooky Lighting, and the shades are handmade by Angela Constantinou of Cocoon Home. The fabric is by Penny Morrison.

The blinds offer privacy all year round, shade in the spring and summer, and a sense of warmth and coziness in the winter. The bold geometric fabric is by Raoul Textiles for George Smith. The green is one of Butter's favorites. "All greens go together, but not all greens are created equal." Though the various colors and patterns in the two rooms could easily skew zany, "somehow they work in harmony." Many of the fabrics, which have similar levels of saturation and intensity, are by Manuel Canovas.

LEFT: Butter added the conservatory to expand the footprint of the house. "This open outdoor area that once lay beyond the double drawing doors seemed a terrible waste of space. A conservatory felt like a sensible solution, and it is now the most lived-in room in the house."

OPPOSITE: The black-and-white theme runs throughout the house in subtle but sophisticated ways and via different patterns and materials, including timeless checkered floor tiles. "The hall floor really was the starting point for a lot of the other details that gradually followed on," says Butter.

OPPOSITE: The kitchen table and pair of benches both were made to measure. Butter chose benches for the space as chairbacks interrupted the view across the room and into the garden room. The striped fabric, Sketched Stripe Green, is by Penny Morrison. The brush fringe trim is 704 2.5cm Ruche by George Spencer Designs.

RIGHT: The Dutch door affords a showy peek of the world outside every day. "This view never gets old," says Butter. "It changes all the time with the weather and the seasons. It is particularly pleasing and oddly a great comfort to me, like seeing an old friend after a long time."

OPPOSITE: The shelf and its contents amuse Butter to no end. When asked the usual question about how she keeps everything clean, she has a cheerful reply at the ready: "Occasionally I take everything down and give it a soapy wash and then put it all up again. I am not that concerned with a little dust, so long as the view is a pleasing one and things are tidy!" Black-and-white Staffordshire porcelain dogs have been a favorite collectible for years. "They are like old friends and make me feel as if I am never alone. My real dog, Wafer, is also a superb companion!" If there's an opportunity for a floral moment, Butter pounces to fill blank spaces with stems and blooms.

RIGHT: The Chalcot candlestick lamp, one of a twin, is from Vaughan Designs. The lampshade is handmade by Butter's dear friend Rosi de Ruig. "I adore her green marbled paper. She has made several lovely lampshades for me throughout the house."

Butter has a particular passion for collecting old china plates with botanical prints on them. "I adore the bright green of these together with the mauve accents." Her sister-in-law, Rosie, painted the wall behind the plate rack to lend further detail and color to this little scene.

LEFT: Butter wanted as much floral interest in this room as possible. The pair of brass wall sconces is by Soane Britain. The lampshades were custom-made by Angela Constantinou of Cocoon Home. The antique floral fabric was found online.

RIGHT: Unlike other rooms of the house, Butter's bedroom is kept "intentionally quite calm." The serene space overlooks the garden. "I feel particularly spoiled. It is the very first thing and last thing I see every morning and night," she says.

OPPOSITE: Butter recently renovated this bathroom to make it more luxurious and more her own. "I wanted to include the most heavenly big bath and cover the walls in paneling, wallpaper, and as many floral prints and pretty, old plates as I could possibly squeeze in." The green wallpaper is Small Medallion by Peggy Angus for Blithfield & Company.

LESSONS FOR A LAYERED HOME

FIND WAYS TO REFLECT LIGHT. A dim space in the front hall needed an aesthetic boost. A mirror found at a local antique shop was the ideal fix. It plays an enormous part in adding light and flow to this reasonably narrow area.

CHECK THE CHAOS. For those who also chase the blitz of color and pattern throughout living spaces, seek out patterns and hues that carry the same intensity and saturation. "It works for my aesthetic, and I find it's the thing that keeps different designs working in harmony," says Butter.

MAKE ROOM FOR THE ANIMALS! Butter adds little animal statuettes here and there and everywhere. On a side table, the cow creamers go so well with all the other shades of orange in this room. "I find them and the Staffordshire spaniels very jolly and joyful, and constant companions who need little to no real attention."

STOCK UP ON THE THINGS YOU USE MOST OFTEN. Butter exhibits a great fondness for generously sized vessels and jars, and keeps her eyes peeled for them when out and about. "I love to stuff them full of flowers in the summer and a huge variety of greens at Christmastime.

DITCH THE MATCHY-MATCHY VIBE. In Butter's rooms, one will encounter a variety of chairs: some with exposed legs and some skirted, some old, some new, and nothing too matching. "It delivers a relaxed, eclectic feel, which I think makes guests feel at ease."

FILL EVERY INCH WITH FLOWERS. Even busy spots, like a shelf or tabletop, have tiny pockets of space. Butter fills them with seasonal flowers from the garden.

LET THE SPACE DECIDE WHAT HAPPENS. The rectangular shape of Butter's backyard dictated how the garden was designed. What ensued: two lush side borders and a wildflower meadow in the middle. "I wanted to have as much space for planting as possible, so the borders are generous, which allows for lots of lovely layers of plants."

OPPOSITE: The floral wallpaper is Floral Trail Wallpaper Original by Salvesen Graham. Butter and her daughter Zoe discovered the prints on Portobello Road in London a long time ago. The pink lamps came from a favorite shop of Butter's called Canford & Co Framers. "They are mostly known for their beautiful bespoke frames and prints, but I have also been known to buy quite a bit of antique china there, too."

at home with
SEAN MCNANNEY & SINAN TUNCAY
BROOKLYN, NEW YORK

PERSONAL TASTE

S ean McNanney and Sinan Tuncay's Brooklyn apartment is oozing with personal touches. It is like walking into a curated gallery where the tiniest, corner-hidden details draw you in. Curious tales seem to want to be told. Sean hand-painted the spectacular friezes in the office and living room, and I made a mental note to find a way to try this technique sometime, perhaps with some professional help. Collections are everywhere you look; they are little homages to memories and places. On the ground, small scatter rugs are deftly arranged to run down the hallway of the railroad apartment like stepping stones. On the fridge, there's a diorama, but that's just one wondrous thing about that room. There are treasures and mementos hanging all over the walls and something for the eye to feast upon no matter where you look. Like in a Parisian house museum, each time you enter the same room, something new catches your eye.

OPPOSITE: On the living room walls, the paint color is Turner's Yellow by PPG, a color inspired by Nancy Lancaster, a decorator who popularized English country-house style. An andiron turned sconce by Christopher Dresser is suspended on the wall. Its twin hangs above the other end of the sofa.

Sean, a textile designer and the founder of Saved NY, has been a denizen of the apartment, which is in the heart of Williamsburg, for over fifteen years. His husband, Sinan, an artist and video director, has lived here for about seven years. In that time, the surrounding neighborhood has changed dramatically as its popularity with tourists has soared; one never quite knows what eatery or trend-loaded retail space is coming or going next. But if you're lucky enough to exit the busyness of the Brooklyn streets and head indoors to where Sean and Sinan have built a curio-filled home within the railroad-style layout of their fourth-floor walk-up, you might even feel a sense of being transported to another dimension.

Summing up their interiors isn't possible in only one word. There are disparate elements that are incontrovertibly compatible. Here, collections reign. Details get granular if you eye them closely, and themes collide with patterns that reveal timeworn history. Travelers at heart, the couple has collected rugs, artifacts, ceramics, and found objects from all over the world. Scattered across the spaces are cultural representations from Brooklyn to Istanbul, where Sinan is from, and myriad places in between. "It's like a palace but also a dollhouse," says Sinan. Beyond the front door, a naturally lit kitchen enveloped in framed minutiae leaves no breathing room upon its walls. By the time you reach the bright yellow living room, you almost want to double back and start again. Sinan says that it can feel akin to being on the Orient Express: "I feel like we're always traveling when we're at home." Sean adds that it could be Paris, or anywhere that you feel most at home. That's the point, he says. "That's why I have collected things that inspire me and make it feel like we could be anywhere."

By design, Sean has a habit of finding something new every day, whether he seeks it out or it's literally put in his path. His regular sources: eBay, auctions, dealer friends who specialize in antiques and furniture, and Instagram. Also, the sidewalk. Sinan trusts his partner's process of collecting and displaying and says he is a practical editor for the shared spaces. It's motivation for Sean to narrow down his collections. Even more, it's a subtle push toward change and considering different patterns, schemes, and showpieces within the footprint of the beloved apartment so as not to pigeonhole the home into one particular style.

"In the future, we're going to redo the place," says Sean. Inspiration is collected like trinkets. "When I go somewhere else, or when I travel, I think, I'm ready to try that at home for the next phase. I think I want to push myself to something new." What that might look like will be determined when the time is right. But there's a good chance that unlike the rapid changes occurring on streets outside, the changes inside Sean and Sinan's home will effuse unbridled whimsy slowly and arrestingly in their own way.

> *"I have collected things that inspire me and make it feel like we could be anywhere."*

The plates are antique Ottoman and Persian, ranging from 100 to 500 years old. The painting is attributed to Giorgio de Chirico.

OPPOSITE: The greenware box was made in Mississippi by a man called Chief. It was a gift to Sean from his mother. Inside are jewelry bits to make something from, as well as broken antique sealing-wax sticks from Paris. The lamp is nineteenth-century Iznik.

RIGHT: A corner cabinet stores antique Iznik, Ottoman, and Persian ceramics. Frames holding Viennese lace, Ottoman calligraphy, and a BDDW puzzle painting share space upon the wall.

ABOVE: Atop the fridge is a vintage diorama of seashells and corals alongside keepsake vases, statuettes, and sculptures. Behind it is a painting of Sean's mother's family.

OPPOSITE: A seat tucked into the kitchen corner in front of a full gallery wall offers a view of the neighbor's backyard and sounds from Brooklyn's North 9th Street.

52 | THE LAYERED HOME

A shelf display in Sinan's office fuses cultures with Hudson River School paintings and pictures of Turkish movie stars like Türkan Şoray.

LESSONS FOR A LAYERED HOME

ELEVATE AREA RUGS. Assorted small rugs from Mongolia, Nepal, and Turkey are soft souvenirs from world travels and, underfoot, they break up the train-car effect of a railroad apartment or any long hallway.

JOURNEY THROUGH A ROOM. When curating a room means filling in empty spaces, think about where one's gaze inevitably goes. Sean loves to make a moment for the overall first glance, then allow the eyes to travel as if you're reading a story.

COLLECT A COLOR. A flock of azure-toned Chinese parrots and parakeets from the eighteenth, nineteenth, and early twentieth centuries create a riveting spectacle when huddled together on a cabinet in the living room.

KEEP REMNANTS OF THE PAST. An early American plate rack hangs above the kitchen worktop. The walls are stained plaster, which Sean colored after the 1970s wallpaper was taken down.

COMBINE OLD AND NEW. Atop a lamp in the living room (page 47) that belonged to Sean's great-grandmother is a lampshade he created in Istanbul using vintage roller fabrics.

OPPOSITE: Sean's studio in nearby Greenpoint is used for photoshoots, sewing, and appointments. The wall is painted. The canopies came from the Plaza Hotel. The carved bed is 1950s French, upholstered in Mountain Man toile fabric from Saved NY with a matching cashmere pillow. On the bed is a DNR Bricks cashmere throw blanket from Saved NY.

shopping with
ERIC GOUJOU
LA TUILE À LOUP, PARIS

UNIQUE DISCOVERIES

This shop of wonders places entertaining and conviviality front and center. Walk through the door, and, if you're like me, the sense of wanting to plan your next dinner fête will hit you within moments. Eric Goujou sources pottery from across France. No two items are alike—different regions specialize in different designs and methods, and you can sense this decorative stratification as you scan the inventory. Eric's devotion to the artisans, and his adoration for craft, is contagious. I especially love hearing about how pieces can be used for more than one thing in the home, like repurposing a colorful platter as a tray. His favorite items are those with animal motifs. When I visited, I kept returning to the big sets of marbleized dinnerware, which I loved because there's nothing quite like having twelve place settings for when the moment— or spontaneous gathering—strikes. But there is something for everyone, and Eric will make sure you find the thing, or things, that you can't wait to have in your own home.

In the 5th arrondissement of Paris, one will find a beautiful home shop by the name of La Tuile à Loup (this translates to "The Wolf Tile"). Online followers will attest that its Instagram feed is a sheer scroll of delight, but it is nothing compared to actually being present amid the whimsical assemblage of decorative tableware and pottery, much of it unexpected yet beguiling, sourced from across France. It's a captivating retail space, strategically outfitted from wall to wall with fanciful vessels, baskets, and tableware that have been thoughtfully handmade by French artisans.

Everything in the shop pokes a bit of fun at tradition, brings playfulness to the practical, and arouses all the senses. The shop owner and curator, Eric Goujou, spent his formative years in the field of private banking but jumped at the chance to take over the shop in 2006. He was a longtime customer, after all. It was a life-changing opportunity to engage his passions for interior design, craftsmanship, and presentation all at once, and to nurture an inner calling to highlight masterpieces of the country's finest artisans for other devoted customers and curious collectors to discover.

Eric believes that delight can take myriad forms, and that the elation inspired by decorative objects is a feeling to celebrate. It's a brilliant tenet to remind everyone that joyful art can live anywhere inside the home. That's why the merchandise at La Tuile à Loup is so special. From gorgeous spatterware serving platters to teeny animal statues, it's designed to prompt conversation, or at the very least, bolster a feeling of fanciful decorative luxury. Here, colors, patterns, and forms are unexpected and unforgettable, and pieces are meant to receive a place at the table of customers who delight in entertaining. To experience the joy of visiting La Tuile à Loup, just book an appointment online. And even if you know exactly what you're there for, chances are other one-of-a-kind pieces will pull you under their spell.

PREVIOUS: La Tuile à Loup has an abundance of animal representation, says Eric. "Our heritage is rooted in French folk arts. Looking around gives the impression of a scene from a toile de Jouy or Marie Antoinette's cottage at Versailles. I see La Tuile à Loup as an idealized countryside." These terrines are oven-safe and ideal for cooking hearty, wintry dishes. But their ornamental nature makes them attention-grabbers, too. "Place one on a dining table as a centerpiece, or display a collection of terrines in different sizes on shelves in the kitchen or dining room," Eric suggests. He appreciates that the terrines are thoughtfully crafted far beyond the city by a talented artist who is also an excellent cook. "My atelier visits are always a joyous occasion. We spend countless hours sitting at the table, and then I take a few days to recover when I return to Paris."

LEFT: Customers of La Tuile à Loup are informed, says Eric. "It's common for our customers to have done their homework before their visit. Oftentimes they are already aware of what's in store thanks to social media or admiring something they saw while visiting a friend or family member." To help steer customers toward pieces that might resonate with their personality and household, Eric asks specific questions like whether they entertain, are drawn to color, love animals, or have children. From there he pulls pieces for them to choose from.

ABOVE: The animal platters and covered dishes at La Tuile à Loup are museum-worthy. "It is the most significant collection I am proud to carry and is a wonderful modern expression of folk arts based on observations of animals in the countryside," says Eric. Though the pieces are oven-safe and perfect for serving food, he also relishes the idea of displaying the foxes, horses, or chickens in a gallery wall or on a plate shelf. Customers fancy collecting the beautiful creatures, too.

OPPOSITE: Though the many platters exhibit a variety of patterns, they were all made by the same artisan, says Eric. He believes that every household needs a few platters; decorative and practical, they are ideal for sharing food with loved ones but also an option when a tray is needed. "A platter can be placed on a pile of books on the coffee table, or on a console or side table." Or take inspiration from the shop and create your own gallery wall with a collection.

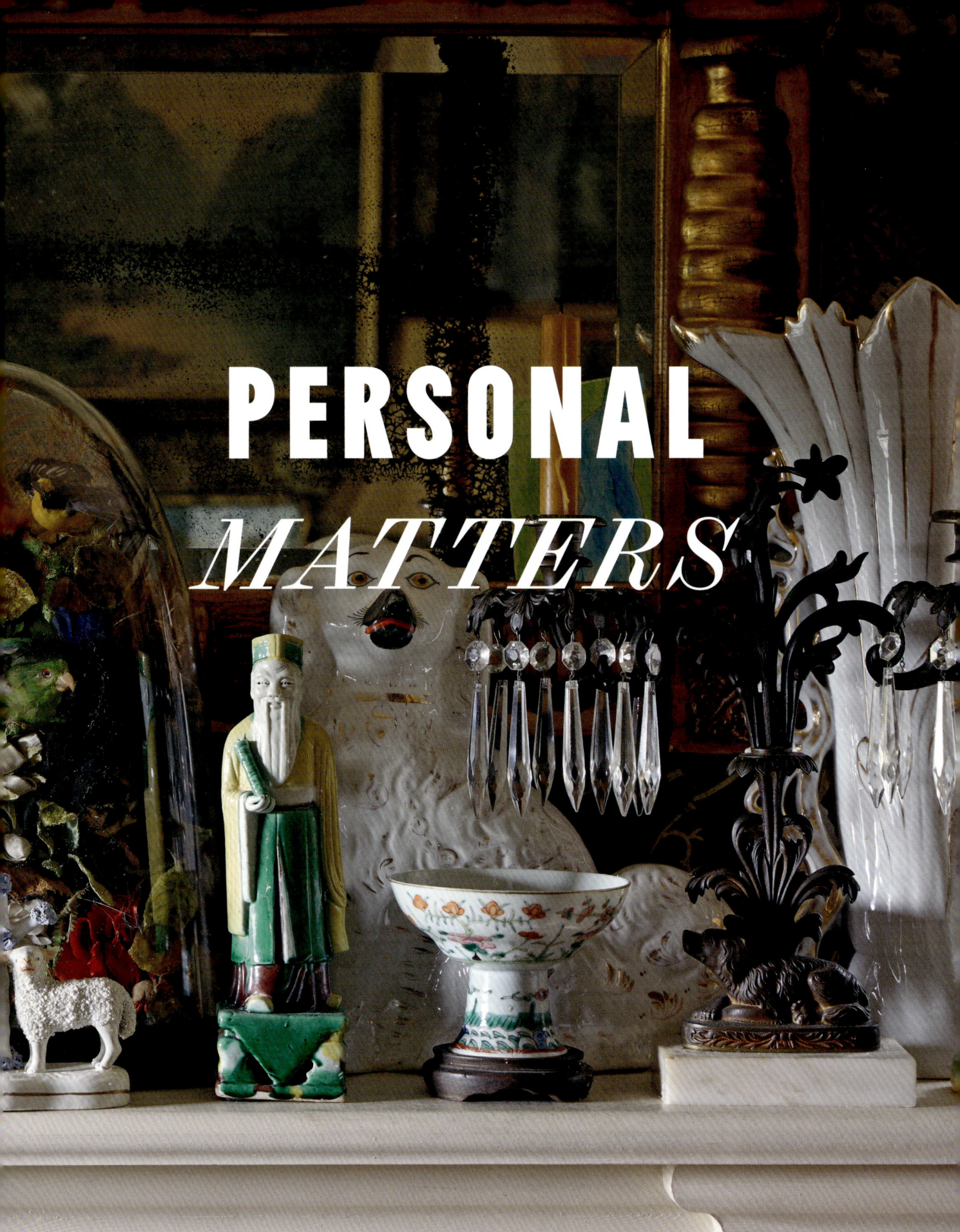
PERSONAL
MATTERS

FIND MEANING IN YOUR SURROUNDINGS

My favorite homes are filled with personality and signs of life. I appreciate the detritus of everyday living and tend to avoid spaces that feel too clinical. I find it comforting to have a few piles of newspapers and magazines lying around to read on the weekends. I enjoy having a beautiful Imari porcelain bowl by the door to corral keys, last week's theater tickets, and postcards from friends. And saving our nephew's drawings and keeping family photos and other paper ephemera tucked into the corners of picture frames throughout the house. If our homes are reflections of ourselves, this is one of the simplest ways to bring that picture into focus. This layer of personality creates a feeling of contentment one can't find anywhere else in the world.

  When I was growing up in suburban Michigan, my family's home featured plenty of framed family photos dotting the top of my great-grandmother's piano and hung proudly, salon style, on a portrait wall. These early memories of infusing meaning into our living spaces imprinted a desire to not shy away from opportunities to reflect our loved ones in our homes. Oftentimes, these elements are removed during shelter magazine shoots to declutter a space, but these are the things I desire to see, to really understand who inhabits these spaces. These familial elements create texture and memory, ensuring that your home is uniquely yours and not lifted from the pages of the latest design magazine or furniture catalog.

at home with
AMBRICE MILLER
OUTSIDE OF BURY ST EDMUNDS, UK

LIVING WITH COLLECTIONS

Every room in Ambrice Miller's home features incredible vignettes, curated collections, and compelling artwork, seemingly on every tabletop surface and wall throughout. It feels sweetly unpredictable yet coordinated in how it all comes together. One thing I noticed was Ambrice's unfettered approach to hanging art. Nothing feels overly precious or too measured, and there's a sense that things can and will change if you blink. I love how Ambrice promotes the idea that art, and collecting, is not just for one type of person or group. Students, young families, solo collectors, and everyone else has the right to chase the feeling of discovery, because what we bring into our homes is an extension of who we are as people and the places we've been or want to go. I can see how this notion is vital to Ambrice and her family, how living with art and objects of fascination (no matter what their shape or history) is supremely good for promoting happiness.

"When I group similar items together, it feels like different artists' or cultural takes or interpretations on the same thing."

The bronze heads featured on the table are a combination of mid-century Benin Bronzes (copies of original bronzes from the Kingdom of Benin, modern-day Nigeria). "They would have been ceremonial or celebratory pieces honoring kings and queens," Ambrice explains. She crafted the large ceramic featured in the middle.

The atelier that is Relic Interiors can be seen as a catchall for old-world finds destined for new beginnings. These rooms are ever-changing in the inventory they hold, sometimes only for the swiftest of stints before they're claimed by a buyer and shipped off to another address. It's the atmosphere Ambrice is used to, relocating these wares to make room for the latest antique market discoveries while assessing how these treasures will resonate with her audience and devoted clientele.

In the atelier, and in her private living spaces, absolutely everything is on display, from the family of chandeliers that dangles above a stately Italian bust, to the array of portraits, to an exotic painted wood peacock situated upon the dining room table (a set design remnant from a 1980s production at the Royal Albert Hall).

Growing up with interiors-obsessed parents was only the beginning for Ambrice. From those beginnings, what bloomed was a deep-rooted love of art and discovery that further evolved into a cultivated shop where fixtures, furniture, and artwork coexist in shambolic harmony waiting their turn on a wall or as a tabletop centerpiece. Ambrice says that the goal of all this goes far beyond feeding a joy of collecting to also noticing something wonderful that's happening with younger generations looking to invest in their own collections. "Everyone remembers the first couple of pieces they bought. Especially if you're a student or if you're a new entrant to the workforce and you buy something with your first couple of paychecks, you're like, wow, it's really something special."

Ambrice believes that the best home life is one filled with color, history, and a touch of the dramatic. Everything is cherished but not so overly precious that it's untouchable. Even with her young son bopping around, he is constantly exposed to the rotating parade of finds and wares that come inside. "Our homes are meant to be lived in. I can't imagine anything worse than not being able to feel like you can properly relax in your own home."

The chandelier was purchased in Paris and was the inaugural piece for this sitting room. "There's a part of me that wishes we used the room more frequently," Ambrice admits, "but equally, because we don't use it often it feels like a treat when we do spend time here, especially when we're hosting friends."

OPPOSITE: Gold frames add a touch of brightness in the hallway leading to the front door. The grassy-hued paint color on the walls is Night Vision by Valspar.

RIGHT: A crowded corner of favorite items becomes a fixation for the gaze, even for Ambrice's son. "When I first got the oil painting, my little boy, who was only just starting to speak, would point to it and call it 'Bubba,' the nickname we use for him. I'm not sure where he got that from or why he started it, but it made me think we all see a little bit of ourselves in art we love."

Ambrice found this patinated sculpture at an antique fair in the south of England. "It's French, from the turn of the twentieth century, and came from an artist's foundry."

LEFT: A dining room wall is full of character and variety. The horse bust is from a shuttered equine shop, where it was used as a tack model. Ambrice says, "I fell in love with it immediately because it looked like a piece of modern art."

OPPOSITE: Two peacocks from a stage set keep vigilant watch. "I originally bought them to sell, but I can't quite bring myself to part with them just yet," Ambrice confesses. "There's something so unexpected about them, especially given their size in a relatively small space."

OPPOSITE: The kitchen mantel creates a shallow stage for more art and vessels. Ambrice purchased the terra cotta vase at an antique fair in the UK.

ABOVE: An understated corner in the kitchen is one of the busiest spots in the home.

LEFT: A combination of paintings collected from travels adds dimensional beauty to a functional area.

ABOVE: Brick and ivy are building blocks of the house, jokes Ambrice. A door hedged by greenery becomes a whimsical focal point. "It was this brick wall and wooden gate that made me gravitate toward the property when I first saw the listing."

OPPOSITE: Amplifying the number of patterns makes this room, known as the Map Room, feel "like the inside of a grandmother's apothecary cabinet," says Ambrice.

LESSONS FOR A LAYERED HOME

BE FLEXIBLE WITH YOUR FINDS. A bust can be both an interior and exterior piece. Ambrice loves the patina that a garden bust displays after years of being in the elements. "That's when you bring it indoors to admire."

CELEBRATE SMALL SPACES. Every space in your home, regardless of size, is an opportunity to surprise or delight a guest. Seek out these opportunities!

TRY "UNMATCHING." Having fun with a bevy of patterns in a bedroom can yield amusingly chic results. Ambrice thinks it's the perfect place to lean into the mantra of nothing matches, therefore everything matches. "I believe this is the foundation of the quintessential 'British cottagecore' aesthetic."

INVITE CURIOSITY THROUGH SHAPES. There's something so tactile about a vase or a pot, or anything with handles, almost encouraging you to pick it up, a merchandising tactic Ambrice employs in her own spaces. It works by forging a more personal connection to pieces that make up your layers. In other words, not everything should just be looked at all the time.

DRESS YOUR DOORS. Even passageways are moments for adornment. Ambrice loves any type of door furniture, as it adds an unexpected but often appreciated surprise.

FESTOON YOUR PARTY TABLE. Ambrice believes that a great tablescape is a service to everyone. "It's a conversation starter if the person next to you is a bore. I think we've lost the importance of setting a table to foster great conversation! Also, my mom loved setting a beautiful table, and it's something we still adore doing together whenever we can. We send each other photos of our tablescapes ahead of dinner parties—friendly competition!"

OPPOSITE: A repository of linens and unusual objects is a go-to spot when creating a new tablescape. "I probably get as excited to decorate a dining table as I do for the actual dinner party."

at home with
JAMES COVIELLO
HUDSON VALLEY, NEW YORK

OLD WORLD

James Coviello started his career as a milliner and then worked in fashion for decades prior to launching his own interiors firm and home brand. I find it intriguing that those who work in fashion almost always also have really strong convictions about their interior style. James originally bought his 1820s farmhouse intending to create beguiling spaces that reflect his deep interest in nineteenth-century decorative objects. As a child, he was constantly making things, some of which have found their way here, and he does a thoughtful job of finding room for many familial nods, from a crowd of cuckoo clocks to old photos tucked into mirrors and drawings from young relatives taped to the fridge.

James is a wonderful "arranger" of things. He told me, "It all works as long as it's symmetrical," which I love. He does mix things up a lot and has a penchant for hanging art, arranging objects, and displaying 3D pieces on tabletops in symmetrical compositions. It does kind of unify disparate items! It's not so simple to source and create an old-world aesthetic that feels livable, but in every room, the mindfully placed furniture and decorative pieces feel like they belong in the present moment. Outdoors, the changing colors and textures of the beautiful garden and pear orchard are reminders that time is constantly leading us toward a new beginning.

OPPOSITE: The dining room, used most often for dinner parties and holidays, is painted in Ochre by Benjamin Moore. "The set of Chinese prints was actually found in Kyoto in a tiny antique shop," James says. "The small black table is a nineteenth-century chinoiserie sewing table with the most incredible dragon head feet I've ever seen!" The dining chairs are Thonet from Vienna with the original labels still on the bottom.

OVERLEAF: The Chinese antique porcelain objects were collected on travels in Asia during James's many years as a fashion designer. The wallpaper is a reproduction of an eighteenth-century French design from Waterhouse Wallhangings called East India.

When the artistic drive to craft, imagine, and create repeatedly makes an appearance early in a person's life, it's always interesting to watch how this drive develops when it's nurtured by experiences, travel, and family support. Early on, James understood that learning and beauty came through the act of creating, and how this autodidactic path would lead him forward. "I was always a creative kid, so I was writing books or drawing or making Super 8 movies and Claymation. It was nonstop, and that was my natural progression."

When the time came, art school in New York City seemed the logical step. But a few years in, James realized that his extracurricular work as a milliner and accessories crafter had garnered interest and an audience, and he made a shift that would plant him inside the world of fashion, where his creations melded with the collections of the finest clothing designers. Though creating hats is now part of his past, this full-scope understanding of the inspired process is an inherent tenet of how James approaches design. The circa 1820 Hudson Valley home (with additions tacked on over time) that he has transformed over the last twenty-five years is a living project and one that has been fueled by a different but equally buoying interest that grew apart from his fashion career.

Enriching the personal living spaces around him meant learning about nineteenth-century decorative arts, material culture, and the vast range of periods as well as styles of furniture and architecture. "I really educated myself, but this is just a personal passion," James says. But then he joined Instagram and started sharing pictures of his home's historically rooted yet resolutely cozy interiors and found quite quickly that another audience was giving attention to his design work, which this time was "purely for

"I really like a room to have a feeling of nostalgia. Almost like you feel you've been there before."

ABOVE: James keeps his dried herbs and spices in a corner of the kitchen along with a mortar and pestle. The white bowl is reserved for onions, garlic, and shallots. Asian pears from the garden fill the small bowl.

OPPOSITE: Though James has a design studio in Hudson, he loves taking in the beautiful view of the Taconic Hills outside his kitchen window. "When I am working from home, this is where you will find me!"

ABOVE: The kitchen was an early nineteenth-century addition that was revamped in the 1950s. "This space was totally gutted down to the studs and redone in a style that felt more appropriate to the original house," says James. Because he is an avid cook, more modern appliances were added. "I like the contrast with the antique surfaces and fittings."

OPPOSITE: The shelving on the left in this butler's pantry was original to the house. James added the sink and marble counter. It's in here that James washes and stores his collection of delicate nineteenth-century plates. Heavy pots and pans are kept at a distance and washed in the kitchen sink instead.

ABOVE: An antique girandole with original crystal prisms stands behind a collection of black nineteenth-century chinoiserie papier-mâché objects.

OPPOSITE, LEFT: These nineteenth-century candleholders with gilded wooden Chinese panel fragments are mounted on a silk fabric frame. They are from a cottage in Newport, Rhode Island.

OPPOSITE, RIGHT: The china closet is nineteenth-century Anglo-Indian. It was found in a shop in Hudson, New York. In it, James stores his Spode china along with Chinese porcelain from travels around Asia.

the joy of nineteenth-century interiors." When the pandemic hit, James kept his attention on perfecting his surroundings in ways that felt historically on point but thoroughly him. Now others were turning to him for help with their own domiciles. One creative director in the fashion world sought his help in transforming their woodland hideaway, a project that has since appeared in *Vogue*.

For James, embracing interior design as a line of work was a long time coming but a logical progression from his days working in the fashion industry in New York City. His private spaces explode with whimsical and quirky arrangements, from cuckoo clocks to taxidermy to glassware and statuettes, as well as with curious layers and choice pieces from the past that feel stylishly appropriate. An unfaltering curiosity continues, but so does an allegiance to the objects and furniture that have been discovered over the years. When he finds something that feels like it belongs, he knows it. "Eighty-five percent of the furniture I have in my house I've had for over twenty years. I'm into tradition. And nostalgia. I like the idea that this is what my house looks like, lovingly built over time, and that when people come here, it's as if they breathe a sigh of relief . . . that this feels right. This is James's house. And I feel like it's like my own tradition."

Equal parts library and sitting room, this room is used often, especially in the colder months when the fire is roaring. Says James: "I am an avid reader and love to peruse history and design books, of which I have many, especially on gardening and nineteenth-century interiors."

The bathroom is painted in tones by Benjamin Moore: The walls are Bone White, the wainscoting is Old Salem Gray, and the trim is Crown Point Sand.

This primary bedroom is the largest and sunniest room in the house. To keep it feeling comfy both day and night, James chose warm, compatible paint colors. The walls and ceiling are Bone White by Benjamin Moore, and the doors and trim are Antique Yellow by Old Village.

LESSONS FOR A LAYERED HOME

KEEP A CAMERA HANDY. As someone who hunts constantly for everything from furniture to filler, James has learned to take pictures of interesting things whenever they cross his path. "I have this big library of images I can quickly reference when working with clients."

TRY COMFORTING COLORS. Creating an alluring atmosphere can be helped along by using paint colors rooted in the past. For the sunny primary bedroom, warm colors with a nod to the historic seemed right. "I really like a room to have a feeling of nostalgia, almost like you feel you've been there before," says James.

EMBRACE THE PAST. Broaden your scope to beyond what's contemporary. In a historic home, sourcing vintage wallpaper patterns is suitable if you're aiming to capture a truly authentic look. Case in point: On a stair landing hangs vintage paper that dates back to the 1920s.

GATHER LOVED ONES. A bookshelf is a perfect place to pool remnants of history, especially the family kind. In the living room, these include a self-portrait James made in high school and, on the top shelf, a teeny photo of his great-grandfather on his maternal side from Basel, Switzerland. The framed drawing, by James's boyfriend, Erik, is of a fantasy creature combining two of James's favorite creatures: his dog, Maurice, and Sasquatch.

GIVE YOUR GALLERY WALL A THEME. As an homage to the Hudson Valley, where he lives, James created a gallery wall in his sitting room devoted to the Hudson River School of painters. "It is a collection of lithographs and paintings in this style, all from the nineteenth century and in their original frames."

OPPOSITE: On a shelf above the bed sits a pack of English nineteenth-century Staffordshire spaniels and poodles. "I have been collecting these figurines for many years and have larger pairs on each of the mantels in my living and dining room," James says. The paint color on the walls is Shelburne Buff by Benjamin Moore.

shopping with
ALICE MINNICH
LARGER CROSS
OLDWICK, NEW JERSEY

LIFE IN THE COUNTRY

Alice Minnich worked for ages in the New York City interior design industry and is an expert in blending traditional and English country motifs. A few years ago, she traded city life for more agrarian landscapes and launched a retail shop within a newly renovated Victorian farmhouse. (Fun fact: The town of Oldwick, New Jersey, where Larger Cross is located, is home to projects by Albert Hadley, including the home he designed for tastemaker Nancy Pyne, for which Pyne Hollyhock fabric by Schumacher is named.)

The shop is set up to be part home and part retail and succeeds as a repository for beautiful collections for the house and garden. It's a joy to visit, like popping into the comforting spaces of a friend you've known for a long time.

"It's all about the feeling of sophistication combined with the practical."

Alice credits the shop's hominess to its combination of soothing wall colors and the refreshing rotation of interesting new pieces and antiques, which give the space heart and soul.

A hulky sign standing guard outside of Larger Cross reads: Country House Antiques & Essentials. Just one hour west of Manhattan, the store is located in a charmer of a town bestrewed with historic homes, rolling hills, horse farms, and expansive old estates.

Alice's mission in founding the shop was about celebrating the allure of objects—antiquated, new, and essential—that define the spaces, domestic hobbies, and pleasures of life.

"It feels like the items in my house, and that's how I approach displaying them," says Alice. In one corner, an assembly of blue Canton china and twin vessels grabs attention, along with eternally chic cabbageware and kitchen dressers filled with serving pieces and porcelain. Also, the best design books awaiting their next coffee tables. "Merchandising, my favorite part of running the shop, is trying to make everything on offer look cohesive and curated, but very simple and gracious," says Alice.

She chose fresh colors and finishes for the shop to create a space that is personalized and polished. Bill Totten, a local decorative painter, is behind the trompe l'oeil wall treatment, a faux limestone technique on the mantel, a naturalist painting within the fireplace, and the additional mix of comfortably balanced colors. What you won't find here: anything modern or contemporary, or any trendy tchotchkes. It's simply not how Alice curates. What you can expect is a mix of new and old heavily influenced by beloved and timeless genres, à la a chic casserole of primitive American and English country antiques, bolstered by wares that look like they've been flown in from Martha's Vineyard and quaint hamlets around New England.

Alice says, "It's all about the feeling of sophistication combined with the practical, like hotel silver with a willow basket, a humble thing with something fancier. I love that mix of high and low." But not everything is necessarily old-school or strictly meant as decor. Customers also turn up for the rotating ensemble of evergreen and seasonal essentials aimed at cooks and gardeners.

As for the shop's moniker, it's rooted in the pastoral surroundings: It was plucked from Larger Cross Road, a country road about ten minutes away.

ABOVE: Used alone or with other patterns, this cabbageware from Portugal always proves fun and versatile for the dining table. "Food looks really delicious against green, to boot!" says Alice.

OPPOSITE: Stems are a regular part of the shop scenery. Flower bouquets from The Collected Garden are often on display in the shop and are available for sale to customers, too. "I also bring flowers from my garden or wildflowers picked while walking my dogs," says Alice. "There is always something green and living in the shop. It's a small detail that makes a big difference."

FOLLOWING, LEFT: Traditional blue and white has been a feature of the shop from day one. "I don't give a fig about trends," Alice says. "I like what I like, and thank goodness there are kindred spirits out there who love similar, classic things!"

FOLLOWING, RIGHT: Shelves are constantly restocked for curious customers. According to Alice, "Sometimes they leave with a major piece and other times, a cleaning brush for the kitchen or a bar of soap; a pick-me-up purchase, a little something pretty to brighten their day."

at home with

GEORGIA TAPERT HOWE

LOS ANGELES, CALIFORNIA

DECORATOR DELIGHTS

I love how Georgia Tapert Howe utilizes color in a very subtle way in her family home. Her approach to piecing together her own living spaces differs from how she crafts interiors for clients, but it's a striking example of following a feeling and trusting that a look will come together. So many things in her home are relics of other places and times in her life, touched by the hands of relatives or coming from homes she's lived in before. Her dining room is a standout in terms of finding the right shade of green, and her living room is a master class in mixing textures. I admire Georgia's effortless style, her respect for the classical architecture of the home, and the way the interior feels collected and sophisticated but also inviting, comfortable, and easy to move through.

OPPOSITE: The inky mantel is original to the house and was painted using Black Panther by Benjamin Moore. The painting is by Ethan Cook. In front of the fireplace, you'll find a pair of vintage Danish armchairs. "I love them just as much today as when I bought them ten years ago," says Georgia.

"I'm a shopper," says Georgia, an interior designer based in Los Angeles. Until 2011, when the West Coast called, Georgia was a full-time denizen of New York City, and she now splits her interior design business between the two. Georgia's style leans traditional, but with a twist of the playfully practical. For clients, she follows the styling principle that their living spaces should reflect their personalities. But at home, in the historic circa 1921 Georgian abode she shares with her family in the neighborhood of Hancock Park, buttoning down her own interiors involves fairly steady contemplation. "I always say that in some ways it's harder to do your own house because I appreciate so many different styles of furniture and textiles."

Georgia explains that it can be difficult to stay the course when dressing her own living spaces and to quell the urge to shop, given her exposure to ceaseless and inspiring offerings in the design world. "Because I see so much, I get tired of the stuff in my own house and want to swap it out. It's not always great for the pocketbook." If the urge hits, and something resonates, a place can certainly be found for it. "When I was growing up, my mom always had beautiful things. If she was on vacation and saw something like an attractive piece of pottery, she would buy it and just find a home for it." The trait has been passed down. "If I find something that I think is pretty, I don't necessarily feel like I have to have a spot for it. I'll make a spot for it."

As for design trends, Georgia knows that her predilection for color and warmth can stand out. "My aesthetic is not your kind of quintessential California white and beige." But color and coziness are balanced in all projects, both for clients and in personal spaces. This equilibrium can often be attributed to incorporating antiques and vintage pieces. "It keeps things feeling individual and not like the project I did before it," says Georgia. "I like houses that feel warm and layered, homes where you want to know who lives there but it doesn't feel like it's one-note."

The front of the historic Georgian home in Hancock Park.

"If I find something that I think is pretty, I don't necessarily feel like I have to have a spot for it. I'll make a spot for it."

OPPOSITE: What's now a console was previously Georgia's desk. To create it, Georgia cut the stone top into a racetrack shape and placed it on a pair of Lucite bases she found in Palm Beach. The candelabra, made of an ostrich egg, was a present from Georgia's mother.

RIGHT: In the background, a portrait of Georgia by Enoc Perez hangs in the dining room. The paint color is Lichen by Farrow & Ball. "It's an earthy green that almost has a little gray in it so I thought it tied the living room and family room together," says Georgia.

BELOW: A playful sartorial sculpture sits upon the coffee table. Georgia explains: "My husband wears glasses, and when we first met, he wore black-framed ones. I saw these and gave them to him one Christmas. He hasn't worn glasses like this in a long time, but I still love them."

Georgia re-covered a pair of Restoration Hardware sofas in a pale yellow Loro Piana fabric. In wintertime, this room becomes a magnet due to its wood-burning fireplace.

LEFT: On a dining room dresser, a navy blue urn purchased years ago sits between two canvas palms sourced in Palm Beach. "The urn is broken in several spots, but I love it and can't part with it," Georgia confesses.

RIGHT: Tableware is considered for future gatherings around the dining table.

OPPOSITE: A series of photographs by Duane Michals hangs in the dining room. The tablecloth is made from a Muriel Brandolini fabric, and the chairs are mid-century modern.

OPPOSITE: A custom banquette in a kitchen corner is a favored spot for meals. Family photos pepper the walls above.

RIGHT: This artichoke vine pattern is part of Georgia's wallpaper collection with Brier & Byrd, which she cofounded with artist Lia Burke Libaire.

FOLLOWING: In the family room, a makeshift reading nook was crafted in a corner. On the wall and bookshelf is Chelsea Gray by Benjamin Moore, a charcoal color with warm undertones. "When I did the upholstery for this room, I fell in love with the wine color against the paint, so that was the jumping-off point," says Georgia.

LESSONS FOR A LAYERED HOME

TAKE YOUR TIME. Not everything has to be done or purchased at once. Georgia spent years amassing furniture and treasures that eventually had a turn in the family home.

EASE UP. When it comes to Georgia's personal spaces, she believes in not overthinking things. "I just buy what I love and sort of hope it flows. It usually does!"

TAKE A PAGE FROM SOMEONE ELSE'S BOOK. Colorful advertisement illustrations culled from a book called *Pre-Pop Warhol* make for a charming gallery wall.

MAXIMIZE SMALL SPACES. A sleek and stylish banquette tucked into a busy corner offers plenty of seating for eating.

HIGHLIGHT SWEET LIFE MOMENTS. In a sitting area featuring Georgia's statement wallpaper, a quad of images celebrates a personalized household gift. "The art is from a friend, and there is a drawing for each member of our family."

OPPOSITE: In the main bedroom, the walls are covered in parchment paper, and the curtains are cream linen with a camel-colored border. The side chair came from a house Georgia grew up in. For this space, it's been re-covered in a fabric by Rogers & Goffigon. The bed is custom-made and covered in a Carolina Irving pattern.

GO BOLD

Consider a layered home as a sum of parts that create a whole. I like to think about the cadence of the home, how one enters and how one might move through the spaces. How does the natural light draw you into certain rooms? What architectural elements catch the eye? Alternatively, what elements create barriers? In mapping out your space, you'll likely pinpoint some spots that desire calm and quiet and others that beg to be louder, with a shocking color or a bold overscale piece of art. When I was thinking about the progression of spaces in the home I share with my husband, I realized that the primary bedroom called out for something vibrant and full of pattern. This east-facing room is at the end of a long neutral, art-filled hallway, so I turned to references of Parisian rooms where everything is done up in a single fabric. This felt like the right move for a room tucked away on an upper floor.

From having seen them in the designs of Billy Baldwin to David Hicks and from Veere Grenney to Rita Konig, I'd always dreamed of having a big canopy bed. When I saw a new oak-leaf fabric and coordinating grasscloth wall covering designed by Nathan Turner, I knew I had to go for it. With the help of a drapery workroom, I was able to create the most divine rendition. The brilliance of this type of bed is that there's no expensive furniture involved. Rather, it's simply an array of fabric panels hung from the ceiling, and it creates a wonderful cocooning effect. One benefit is that it fosters the sensation of a room within a room, so the space feels quite a bit larger than it is.

Having spent many nights covering design trade shows in Paris over the years, I have stayed in my fair share of tiny bedrooms decked out in naturalist patterns, whether floral, tree of life, or garden motifs, and I always find them comforting and special. A good bedroom should feel like your own personal retreat. For me, climbing vines create the feeling of being high up in a tree house. Of course, I did have doubts every step of the way, but I also knew what I wanted and kept that in my field of vision. There were times when I felt I should back off, but I believe that densely patterned rooms can be restful, calming, and, most important, personal. Finding a pattern that speaks to you is the ultimate luxury and antidote to living in an anonymous box.

at home with
PATRICK "PADDY" O'DONNELL
WORCESTERSHIRE COUNTY, UK

WELL CRAFTED

Paddy O'Donnell is incredibly skilled at doing decorator-y things for less throughout his warm and cozy home. Adding clever, easy-sew pelmets to window tops; gluing tape trim at the upper corners of a room to hide a poor paint job; and being super selective with a limited supply of wallpaper—it's true, you don't need to wallpaper the portion of a wall covered by a massive breakfront that you know you'll never move! These are all par for the course in the English countryside abode Paddy calls home. He never takes things too seriously in a room, a Nancy Lancaster–ism, I believe, and a very English sentiment overall. The way Paddy hangs art and objects on walls creates playful architecture where there might not be any. Look up and you'll see plates exhibited above doorways. Art, candle sconces, and brackets are arranged on the wall in a way that that sets a tone of togetherness through precisely chosen colors (a language he understands so very well).

FOLLOWING: Above the late-Victorian-era dining table dangles a 1960s Hans Kögl wheat sheaf chandelier. The mirror is eighteenth-century Irish gilt. The roman blinds are fashioned from a classic Colefax and Fowler chintz pattern called Tree Poppy. The verdant-toned wallpaper is a discontinued colorway from Colefax and Fowler called Livingstone.

Turn a corner in Paddy's house, and the interior scenery changes. Chromatic values shift, open up, and suddenly invite new patterns, furniture forms, and energy. But shock value is not what's happening within these areas, and it is not Paddy's intention. Here, similar rooms under one roof wear their own color outfits dictated by light, emotion, and purpose, then are lovingly accessorized with artwork, heirloom pieces, and other remnants of time, travels, and memory. And the colors! For visitors, it becomes a curated and comforting maze to explore. Almost too much, and definitely not too little.

The way Paddy embraces hues in truly thoughtful and personalized ways is expected, given his color-curious personality and real-world calling as a color consultant and ambassador for the esteemed Farrow & Ball brand of paints and wallpapers. Though color is his life, Paddy stands by the notion that "different looks will naturally dictate different palettes and considerations."

He encourages clients to think very deeply about their aesthetic ambitions for a room, and all the elements to be used in the space, from flooring to fabrics, tiles, and more. The design vibe will affect how color appears; the same color will feel different in a more minimalist room than in a layered, textural space full of pattern and print.

Ultimately, Paddy says to think about bringing in color later in the design process. "You don't want to be constrained by your color choice. I always talk of color in the room as the glue that unites everything rather than the star of the show!"

Though it rarely gets used, the cupboard in the dining room is full of Spode tableware owned by Paddy's mother. Changes are in store for the storage unit. "I have fabric to make little screens behind the doors," Paddy says.

OPPOSITE: Farrow & Ball's Biscuit, "the most forgiving warm mid-neutral," according to Paddy, coats the walls and trim. A slight yellow lamp casts enough warm illumination for poring over cookbooks or doing a crossword at the kitchen table. The marbled paper lampshade is by Compton Marbling in Wiltshire, UK.

"I'm not one for empty surfaces, but each object holds a little story of time and place, which is so important in any room."

ABOVE, RIGHT: A lamp scored from Homesense is topped with commissioned silk ikat shades by designer Melodi Horne.

ABOVE, LEFT AND OPPOSITE: The surface of a console table is covered in assorted bits and bobs. "I'm not one for empty surfaces," says Paddy, "but each object holds a little story of time and place, which is so important in any room." The pair of bronze lamps was originally intended for a house in Ireland. The painting comes from an antique shop in Tetbury. "It had a lovely Bloomsbury vibe, which is a big influence on me. But alas, no budget for a Duncan Grant!"

"You don't want to be constrained by your color choice. I always talk of color in a room as the glue that unites everything rather than the star of the show!"

Paddy never hesitates to hijack a bookshelf with art. "Because books play such a prominent role throughout the home, sometimes it's nice to break up a bookcase with pictures (occasionally out of necessity and running out of wall space). It's an age-old trope, but I love applying it in rooms where possible."

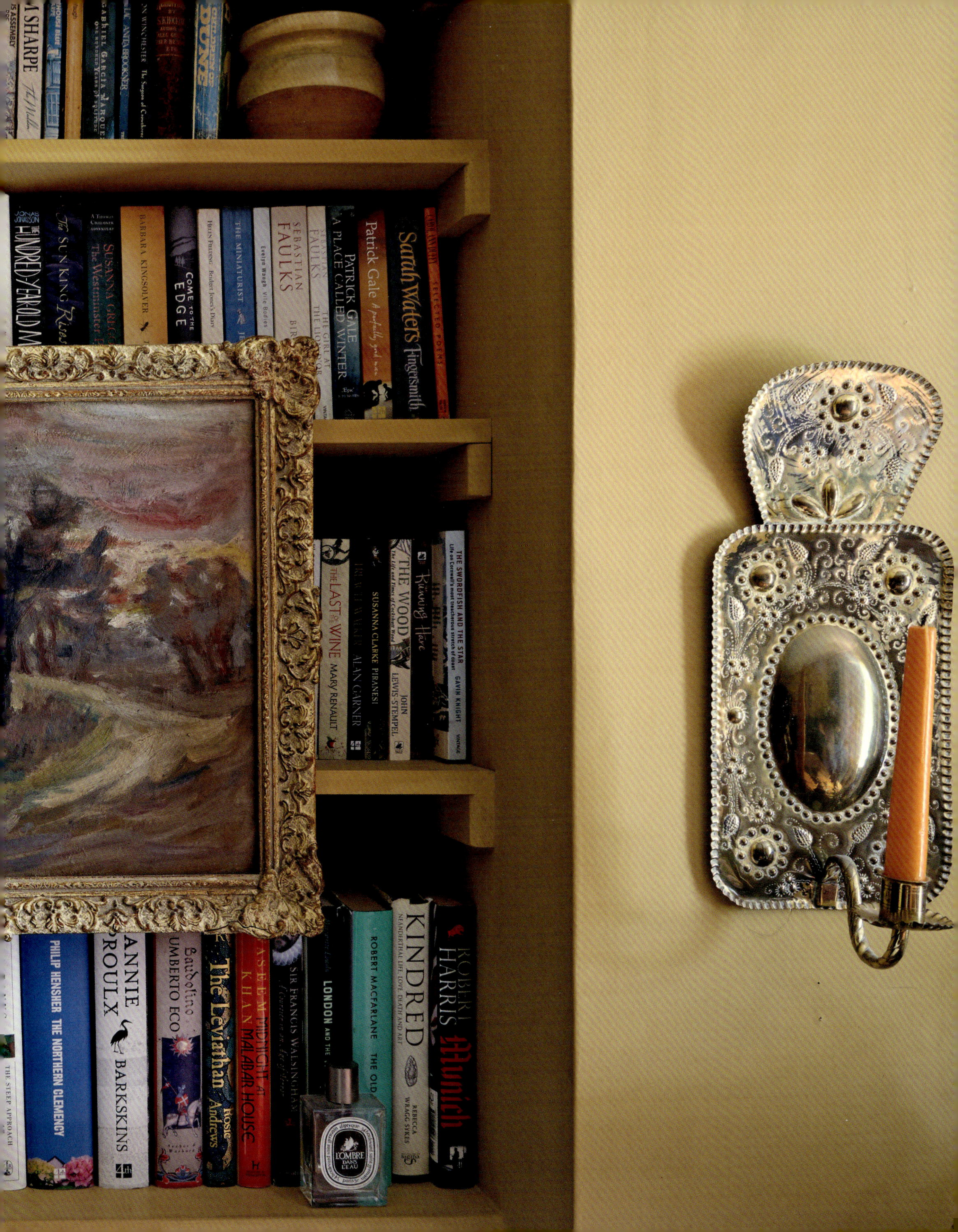
SHARPE
GABRIEL GARCIA MARQUEZ
DUNE
BARBARA KINGSOLVER
SUSANNA GREGORY The Westminster
The Sun King Rises
COME TO THE EDGE
THE MINIATURIST
SEBASTIAN FAULKS
PATRICK GALE A PLACE CALLED WINTER
Patrick Gale
Sarah Waters Fingersmith
SELECTED POEMS
THE LAST OF THE WINE MARY RENAULT
ALAN GARNER
SUSANNA CLARKE PIRANESI
THE WOOD JOHN LEWIS-STEMPEL
Running Hare
THE SWORDFISH AND THE STAR GAVIN KNIGHT
PHILIP HENSHER THE NORTHERN CLEMENCY
ANNIE PROULX BARKSKINS
Baudolino UMBERTO ECO
The Leviathan Rosie Andrews
MALABAR HOUSE
SIR FRANCIS WALSINGHAM
LONDON
ROBERT MACFARLANE THE OLD
KINDRED REBECCA WRAGG SYKES
ROBERT HARRIS Munich
L'OMBRE DANS L'EAU

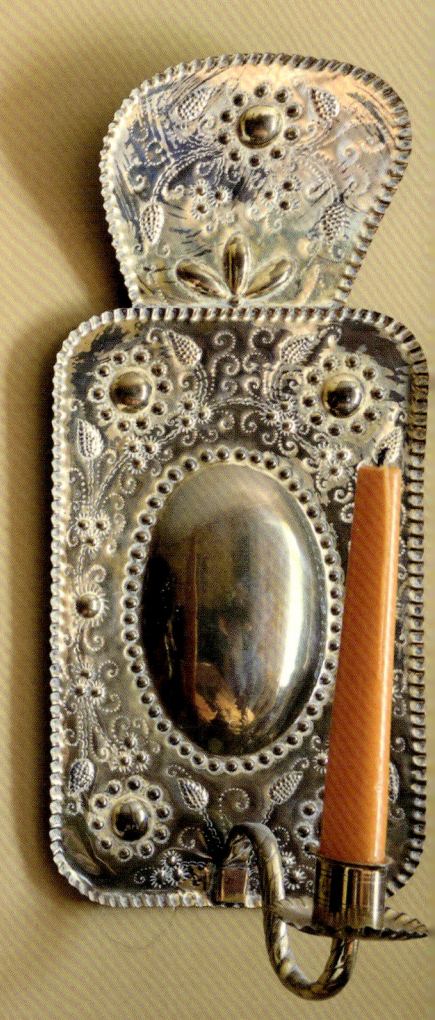

LEFT: The faint pink paint in the hallway is Pink Ground by Farrow & Ball. "I wanted something gentle here but with a little warmth, as the space is all diffused light coming in from other rooms," explains Paddy.

RIGHT: With its diminutive motif, a wallpaper called Hawkbury by G P & J Baker prettifies a tight bedroom corner. "I love small-print papers, as they just create a soft foil for wall dressing with pictures," says Paddy. Framed is an eighteenth-century map of Northumberland on the North East coast of England.

OPPOSITE: A discontinued Farrow & Ball block print called Orleans Stripe envelops the space. Above the tub hangs an assembly of eastern European slipware plates. "They are fairly crude, but I love the way the slip creates these wonderful, feathered patterns," says Paddy.

OPPOSITE: Reading materials are given a large part of the interior real estate. "Books are everywhere in our spaces. From those to read to those for reference, I couldn't be in a room without books!" says Paddy. The shelves are coated in Wainscot, a tobacco-like shade from the Farrow & Ball archive.

RIGHT: On the windows, a striking chintz from Sibyl Colefax & John Fowler affords a chance for colors like brown and blue to be further expressed in the space. The paisley print is Cypress from Howe at 36 Bourne Street. A simple valence on the pelmet features Lewis & Wood linen. A trio of hand-painted nineteenth-century plates expands the floral motif.

OVERLEAF: A favorite fabric called Berber Stripe from Madeaux by Richard Smith brings woolen stripes to the headboard. "I've used this fabric in so many spaces!" says Paddy. The portrait above the bed is an eighteenth-century oil painting in the manner of Jacques-Louis David. "It's utterly charming and exquisitely painted."

LESSONS FOR A LAYERED HOME

SAVE COLOR FOR LAST. The rooms that people decorate for themselves tell very personal stories, and Paddy likes considering how color doesn't need to dictate the narrative from the get-go. "While color is also very personal, ideally, it will come last so as to give you more freedom with everything else."

FOCUS ON THE UNDERTONES IN WHITE PAINT. When choosing colors, Paddy always advises using whites that share a similar undertone to the wall color or vice versa.

BE ADVENTUROUS. Bolder color choices can be great fun, especially with the fifth wall, aka the ceiling. No longer an afterthought, the ceiling is very much part of the decorating repertoire, says Paddy. "At the more subtle level, painting in a 'white' that complements the wall color or going 'off-piste' with a bolder accent color done well can be a triumph and makes a wonderful design statement. You can even mix up the finish, such as using full gloss instead of the go-to emulsion like flat or eggshell."

ZONE IN. If the room contains a niche for a piece of sculpture, Paddy suggests adding a color within the niche to help the piece shine.

TONE THINGS UP. On a bookshelf, Paddy suggests applying two colors, one for the exterior framework and a contrasting color on the interior. "Beyond creating visual interest, it is often just a subtle consideration when shelves are dressed with books and objects!"

OPPOSITE: In a corner of the office hangs a circa 1966 painting by Ukrainian artist Mykola Andruschenko purchased in a Notting Hill gallery. Paddy says, "The colors are just so vibrant, and the picture has a glorious playful quality to it."

THREE RECOMMENDED PRINCIPLES FOR USING COLOR

1. Lighter woodwork and darker walls

2. Darker woodwork and lighter walls

3. One color all over, aka color drenching

TWO WAYS TO GET COLOR TO FLOW IN YOUR LIVING SPACES

1. Pin down a color family. This is a vertical grouping on most color cards from a paint manufacturer.

2. Pick out some stronger colors that complement the chosen family to avoid having the space feeling too bland. Using colors of similar weight—essentially colors of similar strength—gives you more opportunity to introduce more colors into your home!

at home with
INDIA HOLMES
ISLINGTON, UK

HANDMADE FLAT

India Holmes has lived in a world of color, pattern, and play since she was little. It's built into her outlook on the world, and expressed through her work as a designer and creator. She's always interested in fresh options for how her home can look; rooms are spaces for embracing change and instilling opportunities for purposeful inquisitiveness. She has a lot of art gifted by friends, all of it cherished. And much of what is kept hails from somewhere or someone else, as recycling and reuse are extremely important to India's way of living—a philosophy that shows in her commitment to working with a community of conscious buyers, designers, and artisans. The sofa cushions with playing card designs, for example, were made from her childhood bedroom curtains. Her entry is amazing and deserves all the attention it gets. For this space, she had good "tent" reference points and was able to create something magical on a bit of a budget. She's quite skilled at getting at the essence of an idea and executing it herself for less, with her signature wit and whimsy.

OPPOSITE: A lick of loud red paint on the inside area of a recessed window brings a hit of contrast to the pink-toned back wall, which is painted in Setting Plaster by Farrow & Ball. "I have always loved red and pink together, so I thought, What a great way to add some interest to the room: painting the window reveals," says India. "The pink is very subtle, though, sometimes not pink at all, and the red is quite dark, so that the pairing isn't too zingy!" The gilt palm lamp was an auction score. Its twin was put up for sale. "I sold one as the room couldn't quite hold two."

ABOVE: This area is in a constant state of flux, especially after a drinks party. "This tabletop combination changes more regularly than I take the bins out!" says India. The small clay sculpture of an Indian man was gifted to her by an artisan she worked with in Kolkata. The faux malachite is a homemade backgammon board. The glass brick ashtray was a present from a dear friend.

LEFT: For India, staging a space is never done. "This room has had numerous layouts over the years and is due for another any day now! Especially in a small space, I am constantly thinking, there must be a better way around. Hours of moving later, and I am satisfied until I get the itch again."

In the two-bedroom residence of India, the co-owner and creative director of Pelican House, a design studio that produces statement rugs and homeware collections, the first sign that one might be stepping into a winsome portal to somewhere unusually special is apparent as soon as you set foot in the entryway.

Strikingly theatrical, the room evokes the spirit of a homemade circus. Above, a treatment of red and white stripes radiates across the ceiling, with the walls drenched in a vibrant blue-green shade. Disparate patterns, stripe widths, and chromatic tones unite largely in part to the tasseled bunting, which is equally a visual distraction from the bold ceiling, and a quiet harmonizer for the busy space.

These small yet substantive decorative details hold similar sway in every room India has designed, constructively bringing order and alignment to rooms where color, pattern, objects, and textures massively converge. India is an avid collector of anything that strikes a chord. "Like a magpie drawn to shiny objects, I have an insatiable love of decorative objects, ceramics, paintings, fabrics—anything and everything handmade or just beautiful to look at. I am a total sucker for souvenirs and trinkets. During wonderful trips abroad, I have always made sure to fly out with half a suitcase free!"

As India is also an avid bargain hunter, nearly everything inside the house was some kind of deal, like the burly haberdashery with twenty-four drawers scored from a nearby auction house for £300.

As a tenet of good living, India advocates for the staying power of furniture and objects within living spaces. "Once something has served its purpose, I often resell it and buy what needs to go in its place. Where possible, I like to sell and rebuy within the same price point, creating my own cycle of free design—these being secondhand objects to begin with—and buying secondhand or antique in some cases."

India's personality plays out in the heavy influence of color and pattern that imbues each space. The default is layering patterns, a reflex that is informed primarily by gut feeling and a penchant for taking chances. For anyone looking to loosen up their pattern-mixing skills, India says color can be a good reference to use as a guide. "If you know you love a pattern and every time you look at it, it makes you happy, the likelihood is it will fall into place with the rest of the patterns in your house."

"If you can marry and align colors from two different patterns, you can put almost anything together."

OPPOSITE: In the bedroom, red, yellow, and green are thoughtfully combined across a range of patterns and motifs. "I have always loved red and yellow together," says India.

FOLLOWING: The zippy yellow extends into the bedroom. Though the walls and vanity match "in essence," zooming in reveals more minuscule details. "The yellow walls are covered in a yellow painted Xuan paper with a white slub silk voile laid over the top, which is a de Gournay product called Dupion. It can be customized to any color!" says India. Beneath the chair rail, a sanded Xuan paper features hand-painted horses. "The design is based on an antique Chinese screen I once saw that was then brought to life by de Gournay."

ABOVE, RIGHT: At just 5 square meters (nearly 54 square feet), the petite terrace with built-in seating is aptly sized for outdoor assemblies. "It's perfect for me, the pooch, and a few friends to have lunch," says India. Constructed of composite material to combat the elements, the surround is festooned in a vibrant shade of green, Dulux 70GY 30/254.

RIGHT: Tiny collections take up minor patches of real estate in every room. "They are a mixture of travel trinkets, often shells I have found, and pretty-looking rocks!" explains India.

A table that looks hoisted by giant thread spools left a strong imprint on India when she first spotted it at vintage mecca Studio & Store. "It was one of those things where you think about it endlessly for days until finally you give in and buy it!" On the left wall, a framed drawing of a small wild boar is India's favorite artwork of all time. "It was made by my talented mother, and I adore it."

LEFT: A gallery arrangement featuring unexpected motifs fills a wall. Below, a cushion hand-embroidered with raffia made by India while at de Gournay.

RIGHT: "I love open shelves," says India. "It makes sense to be able to see all your favorite glassware and ceramics—they won't bring you the same joy hidden in a cupboard. Only dust is my enemy here, and actively being reminded that you can never have enough glasses!"

OPPOSITE: A storage haberdashery scored at an Islington auction house allows for thorough organization of India's expansive collection of arts and crafts materials.

OPPOSITE: The wall of tiles is actually an optical illusion. More specifically, a hand-painted wallpaper inspired by Portuguese tiles that was designed by de Gournay, where India worked before launching Pelican House. "I originally designed the tiles in collaboration with Alessandra Branca, then when drawing them to fit my kitchen, added in some additional elements like the fruit bowls." The wallpaper features an extra-strong lacquer finish, making it durable for use in the kitchen.

RIGHT: A serious shade of navy, Stiffkey Blue by Farrow & Ball, was selected once the marble had been chosen for the kitchen. Upon reveal, it was more vibrant than India had planned, but it set a chromatic bar for the matching tiles to accompany it.

LESSONS FOR A LAYERED HOME

RETURN TO PATTERNS YOU LOVE. There are always those fabrics or patterns that you adore timelessly. Enjoy what moves you, says India. "If I had to pick one designer whose patterns capture my personality, I would always come back to Josef Frank. I have so many of his prints in my house, and I never get tired of them. They are all really busy, with lots of color and lots going on." She also loves flame stitch, and, although it's not exactly a pattern, she has a soft spot for moiré, too, especially on walls. And, of course, block prints. "Block-printed fabrics, picked up on my many trips to India, will always be seen in multiples in my home," she says. "You can often mix and match many different ones and they look great alongside each other."

TEST YOUR COMFORT ZONE. If you are drawn to a particular pattern, go ahead, give it a try. It might be the very thing you need for your space, says India. "I love layering different patterns, I only find them uncomfortable if I don't like the pattern! Color, of course, plays a big part. If you can marry and align colors from two different patterns, you can put almost anything together."

INSPIRATION HIDES IN PLAIN SIGHT. India loves how even the smallest details of life can inspire new designs. "Quite a few times I have been looking at a pavement in London or elsewhere and realized that some of the manhole covers have beautiful patterns on them, especially the old ones! Our Pelican House Hati rug is based on a run of railings I used to drive past every day on my way to the de Gournay embroidery studio when it was based in Ranihati outside of Kolkata. I always loved the way they look, so I took a picture a few years ago and recently translated it into a rug."

DON'T GET MIRED IN PARTICULARS. Overthinking how it all comes together isn't productive, says India. "I know that if I like things enough, they'll just work."

CELEBRATE WHAT CAME BEFORE. In the main seating area (as seen on page 155), Alice in Wonderland fabric from India's childhood bedroom curtains was repurposed into cushy pillows. The sofa was in India's father's first ever flat. "We should all embrace the cyclical movement of possessions," she says.

OPPOSITE: In the entrance area, striped bunting makes a statement while also acting as a decorative unifier. "It's what I like the most," says India. "It ties everything together, when most of it wants to clash! It also averts one's eyes from the uneven painting of the ceiling."

at home with
KATE DONOVAN & LESLIE JOBLIN
WATER VALLEY, MISSISSIPPI

PERSONAL AND PAINTERLY

There's an energy and excitement brimming forth at Kate Donovan and Leslie Joblin's pastoral home in Mississippi, and that has everything to do with their combined fearlessness when it comes to paint. Trained as artists and academics, Kate having studied fine art at RISD and Leslie having completed a dissertation on the Bloomsbury Group and domestic living, both bring a wealth of knowledge and historic references to what they're doing. Whether it is a wall, door casing, cupboard door, furniture, or even a ceiling fan, they say, Why not paint it? Everywhere you look, there is a personal, bespoke touch, lovingly hand-painted by these two, creating a true handmade home.

They bring color and pattern to the forefront, utilizing textiles on furniture and hanging them on walls as artwork. Color radiates throughout the home. I don't think there's a white wall in the place. Kate and Leslie also showcase their collections, evidence of lives well lived and traveled, everything from American baskets acquired in Pennsylvania to elements from nature gathered and arranged beautifully. Every surface, object, and moment within Kate and Leslie's home showcases the couple's love of collecting, entertaining, music, and sourcing local art from their close-knit community.

OPPOSITE: In the background foyer, a thin rustic farm bench awaits visitors. The wall color is Afternoon by Sherwin-Williams. On the wall, a cluster of artwork is on display. The brass magnolia plate on the wall and ceramic book atop the credenza are by Kate.

As anyone who's ever lived in a shoebox apartment knows, smallish domiciles limit what you can have around you. "Breathing room" can take different forms—negative space, scaled-back colors, or minimal layers, for starters—in order to maximize square footage. For artist and illustrator Kate, memories of a tiny New York City studio apartment filled with matchbox paintings are cherished, but there's a pleasant freedom in having more room now to personalize with relaxed abandon—also, in having a partner who brings a distinct expressive vibration to shared living spaces.

The Craftsman bungalow with the big porch in Water Valley, Mississippi, about an hour south of Memphis, came into the purview of Kate and her partner, Leslie, a communications specialist, through a friend and through fate. Hints of mirth, like the cat-head post on the front porch, caught their attention. They ran with it from there. Both are quick to say they're not tied to any particular design style, but they are devoted to the intuitively collaborative results of what fills their spaces. "It's really improvisational," says Leslie. "The first rule of improv is 'Yes, and . . . ' If someone throws something out there, you have to pick it up and build on it. And I feel like that's how we are."

For interior rooms, this has meant carefully chosen colors, hand-painted details, and a convergence of organic and wispy florals that meld nicely with graphic patterns. "Paint has been our main medium. We've repainted every room in the house but one," says Kate. How this translates: The perfect glowy shade of yellow in the living room to make it feel bright and open. A dark navy blue bedroom to invite powering down. A dining room dressed in a hue of pinky brown that subtly changes color in the light. And a library with green walls and a blue ceiling that feels earthy and grounding.

The duo used color to bring definition to the home's 2,000 square feet of living space and to organize different zones. Then there are the arrangements of art, textiles, found objects, and personal collections that fill in the gaps. One shared mission in their home: to make acting on creative whims as effortless as possible. "We've been trying since we moved here to make art-making even more accessible, just to have things at hand so we use them more. Asking ourselves, How can we make this as easy as just turning on the TV?" says Leslie. The answer is in plain sight: They keep stamps, vases of markers, and conversation-starting objects on display—all to entice them to engage in the creative act alone, together, or with curious guests.

"Nothing is too precious, and any surface has the potential to become an experiment in color or pattern."

OPPOSITE: In the guest room/library, the door and trim are painted in Blue Pot by Memphis-based paint company Farrell-Calhoun and the green is a custom blend of two Farrell-Calhoun colors: Mountain Meadow and Plateau. The floral motifs were inspired by the couple's vintage suzani and the Japanese magnolia outside their kitchen window. The pink and green border is based on a vintage Japanese kimono design, and the exterior border is an abstracted version of a fluted Doric column. Kate says, "Leslie painted all the backs of the shelves, the ceiling, and the trim with Blue Pot and Rocky Mountain (the color of the dining room)—we wanted the library to feel inviting rather than formal."

This main hangout space, dressed in a sunshine shade of yellow called Afternoon by Sherwin-Williams, fills with light in the morning. The cozy roll-arm sofa has moved with Kate from her days in New York. The club chair is from an estate sale, and the pie safe, found at a local antique store, was retrofitted to hide the television and record player. The adjustable Victorian cane chair is from an antiques store in Tupelo, as is the tapestry stool. The walls are decorated with a blend of treasures including vintage baskets, an antique suzani, a linoleum carving by Leslie, a very meta David Hockney poster, and art by Ron Liberti, Taylor Loftin, Pannawat Thamutok, and Kate.

ABOVE: An ever-expanding record collection is stored on a bookshelf. Above it is a Rimbaud portrait by local artist and friend James Kane. The watercolor is by another local artist and friend, Robin Whitfield. Vintage pieces include the plate, cat painting, pansy print, and majolica vase. The Kew Gardens print is from a trip to London, and the African basket is from an estate sale. The lamp, from Leslie's grandmother's house, got a fresh coat of Blue Pot paint, the same color as the study doors.

OPPOSITE: A compact corner doesn't need to lack power. "I used a lot of music prints and primary colors in the mattes, frames, lamps, and decorations to amp up the energy of the space," says Leslie. The quartersawn desk, found at a Pennsylvania thrift store, was a birthday gift to Leslie from Kate.

Books of fiction are organized alphabetically, and "bite-size" options like poetry, essays, and cultural criticism are strategically placed on the lowest shelf, says Leslie. "It's in case any overnight guests want something short to dip into. I'm always curious to see what people pull out. Something on the evolution of gardens? How Liz Phair changed indie rock? The secret life of dictionaries?" A butterfly drawing by a friend, Izzy Thornton, shares shelf space.

ABOVE: A combined book nook and guest bedroom took shape around a daybed and stocked shelves. "The warm wood makes this area feel almost cabin-like," says Kate.

RIGHT: Mementos of sojourns to New York City, a collection of stamps hangs in a vintage typesetter's drawer. "When Kate lived on East 18th Street in NYC, my visits would entail a pilgrimage to Veniero's, an Italian bakery, and Casey Rubber Stamps in the East Village," says Leslie. "I was like, 'Who needs this stamp of a cat putting his boots on?' And my next thought was 'I do.'" Leslie uses the stamps for planning, travel logs, and postcards. "They're great conversation starters. When we have events like the Art Crawl, where hundreds of strangers are coming through the house, sixteen-year-olds and sixty-one-year-olds alike will get curious and chatty."

OPPOSITE: One of the first things Leslie and Kate bonded over was cookbooks. Above the bookshelf, pots hang on a hand-forged rack from a blacksmith in West Virginia. There are prints of two favorite local catfish joints: Ajax Diner and Taylor Grocery. The fruit etching and little still-life paintings are by Kate, the cross-stitch Mississippi map is from a junk shop, and the chicken print is from North Carolina. The paint color on the wall is Hidden Glade by Farrell-Calhoun.

RIGHT: A while back, Kate started painting designs on tapers like this one by using a special shelf-stable wax. The silver candlestick belonged to her grandmother, and the dishes, cup, and tray are collected vintage pieces. The teapot is by Pennsylvania ceramicist Ian Stainton. Kate says, "I bought the pot for Leslie as a birthday gift after she saw it at a shop and said, 'I don't ever think about having tea, but maybe that's because I've never had this specific teapot.'"

The tabletop, covered in an Indian block-print cloth, holds a mix of vintage pieces along with an Italian spatterware dish. The candleholders were purchased at the Charleston house gift shop in Sussex. A love of entertaining is a great reason to collect old pottery and china. "Dishes of different sizes are always useful," says Kate. Including for holding produce that makes it into Kate's art projects. Leslie says, "Kate always thinks that we are out of produce, like onions, lemons, apples, et cetera. I have learned to check the studio, dining room, and porch before making a grocery run, because more than likely the produce has made its way into a vignette for one of Kate's still lifes."

ABOVE: Against a wall painted in Sea Serpent by Sherwin-Williams is an arrangement of found objects including an inlaid wood square from a Victorian-era game table. The ceramic horse is from outside Todos Santos, in Baja, Mexico. "Friends and I went out to a ranch in the middle of the desert for a ceramics class with ceramicist Doña Ramona—this is one of her pieces," says Kate. The long fishing lure was found by Leslie.

OPPOSITE: In the main bedroom, bookshelves from Gothic Cabinet Craft in New York City flank the bed, creating a makeshift nook. The striped pillow shams are from Schoolhouse; the pink ones from Anthropologie. The coverlet is from Coyuchi, and the blue mudcloth pillow is vintage. The lamps are by Visual Comfort. Above the bed hangs a tapestry by Uruguayan artist Maite García Argul. "It was one of the first things we bought for the house after closing," says Kate. "We bought it as a little signal to ourselves that we could live a dreamy life unfettered by too much convention."

LESSONS FOR A LAYERED HOME

FIND YOUR IDEA OF COZY. Once you land on it, add it to every space where it makes sense. For Kate, it's soft lighting and candles in just about every room.

CELEBRATE CREATIVE MENTORS. It goes without saying that Kate and Leslie's approach to decorating is inspired by the Bloomsbury Group and the ethos of what Vanessa Bell and Duncan Grant created at Charleston. "Nothing is too precious, and any surface has the potential to become an experiment in color or pattern," says Kate. "Things can be painted over or changed or moved around. Our home is a lived-in space where we can read and make art, sit in the morning light with our coffee, and snuggle with the cats."

MAKE THE ACT OF CREATING CONVENIENT. In the living room, oversize vases hold not flowers but colorful swirls of pastels, pens, and acrylic markers. The handsome chest in the dining room with its many shallow drawers houses collage materials. "If those materials are buried in the back of the closet, you're just not going to get into them as much!" says Leslie.

IF IT'S MEANT FOR THE FLOOR, TRY IT ON A WALL INSTEAD. "We have more love for rugs and textiles than we have floors, and thus our walls make up the difference," says Leslie. "It works for us—we're both allergic to matchy frames or minimalist spaces. We like the visual interest of a dance of colors, shapes, and textures."

ARTFUL
ARRANGEMENTS

YOUR HOME IS A CANVAS

During my undergraduate fine arts studies, I learned the value of underpainting: sketching out the composition of a painting in charcoal before building up layers of paint to add the right color and texture. A similar exercise is equally useful when it comes to composing the rooms in our homes. I like to remove everything and start with a clean slate. Oftentimes it's helpful to make sketches or create mood boards, but nothing beats good old trial and error, in my humble opinion. I recommend seeing things in real space and time, starting with the upholstered furniture and rug, then thinking about how the room is meant to function and building the foundation with those considerations in mind before layering in smaller items and accessories.

When it comes to hanging artwork, my biggest tip for compulsive art arrangers is to use a small-scale print wallpaper as a backdrop. It hides all nail-hole sins made when busy minds wield busy hammers. My walls are like Swiss cheese based on the number of times I relocate artwork, and having a small-print paper helps cover up any indecision that might come with hanging art, plates, and objects on the wall. I think of each surface as its own canvas, one that we should not feel precious about. If you don't have forgiving wallpaper, a tub of spackling paste and small cans of touch-up paint will do the trick, too.

Whether it's artwork or furniture, I'm always moving things around to accommodate new finds. I think a mantelpiece or wall shelf is a great stage for testing out ideas with objects. Like when underpainting a canvas, I like to see how objects look when grouped together. I like to arrange things and take a step back to see how well they get along. It's nice to see that a deco candlestick might be the right thing to have next to a Turkish vase and a bone box from India. Giving yourself the freedom to play is one of the best ways to engage in a dialogue with your home and create meaningful layers built upon your favorite things.

at home with
SCHUYLER SAMPERTON
LITCHFIELD, CONNECTICUT

LIVING WITH PATTERN

Schuyler Samperton's farmhouse has countless layers. And the house itself is a hybrid of spaces. Its core is from 1828, but some additions can't be dated, and there's no documentation of what was there before. The house isn't symmetrical, which felt uncomfortable for Schuyler at first, but that got her ad-libbing, using what she had from her trove of collected items and heirlooms. The results bring their own hybrid vibe to the spaces. Influences from across the pond abound. There's also an occasional remix, whether a new fabric on a piece of furniture or a new arrangement of collectibles upon a surface, that challenges expected aesthetics, and creates something distinctive. It's very fun to see how this plays out. Every room in Schuyler's home has a dog in it—either a portrait or a figurine. Her guest rooms are welcoming with a dose of unexpectedness, and I find the primary bedroom to be a master class in pattern-on-pattern decorating.

OPPOSITE: In the main bedroom, Schuyler's Floriana pattern in the color Oro wraps both the walls and the windows for a thoroughly seamless look. "It is an exotic take on the typical floral scheme, and the trompe l'oeil craquelure is quite charming."

"I want to live with what I'm creating."

OPPOSITE: Upon a broad round table, a stage for small stacks of photography books, a vintage heirloom shawl colorfully echoes the Serapi rug underfoot. It was the first item bought for the house. "I like things that have a lot of age that are sort of beaten-up and worn, so that dictated the color palette," says Schuyler.

A recurrence of form is a pattern, and in the Litchfield, Connecticut, home of Schuyler, an interior designer and textile creator, pattern runs rampant across the seven bedrooms and three bathrooms. Exactly where the pattern presents itself in each room differs—there's no formulaic or expected approach to where decorative items appear in spaces, but they're all infused with color and with selections from Schuyler's vast personal collection of furniture, fabrics, framed art, and delightfully fanciful objects. Because of her affinity for dogs, she has worked canine portraits and figurines into the scheme of every room. No corner or wall is without a personal touch. In fact, many of the wallpaper designs and fabrics used for pillows and curtains are Schuyler's own, possibly conjured in the convenient workspace located above the garage.

"I want to live with what I'm creating. So it's almost like I'm creating things that I want to see in different rooms of the house as well as trying to use things that we already have."

Pop into any room, look closely at what's around you, and you'll see meaningful pieces affixed to the walls, and vignettes staged in cupboards and on bookshelves and mantels. To Schuyler, everything has a story and a time stamp, and much of what shapes her living spaces came from or was inspired by the things she loves most—family, other places she's lived, travels, and collecting sprees. "When I was younger, my dad was an architect, and my mom was really into design. The lessons I learned from them—about scale and proportion and how to use color and notice color—were just sort of integrated into our daily life. My parents always pointed out to me things like a beautiful color combination on a house or the workmanship on the sleeve of a dress. That's what my family was about."

Parting with objects that have been in the family for generations doesn't come easily to Schuyler. But though things have been stacked away in storage over time, they eventually have their moment among the mix in the living spaces. In many ways, Schuyler's style is like a bridge between the UK and the US—her space is super relaxed in an English countryside kind of way but has a touch of formality seen in traditional American decorating styles. It's tasteful, worldly, fun, and suburban chic.

Schuyler grew up in Washington, DC, and lived in LA for over thirty years, but moving back east in 2017 was like coming full circle. Litchfield is where Schuyler and her partner, Marc, landed and found their historic home, which at its core is resolutely historic, with various additions over the years creating a hybrid layout. If anything, it has the room to showcase more than a few of her favorite things. "I'm super sentimental. I've collected things over the years that I've just stashed away," she says. With this home, Schuyler finally had a place to use everything, including precious pieces inherited from her late parents. "I know they would be so happy that these things found another life with me."

Like many houses in the Northeast, this one is a hybrid. The core of it is circa 1828, and various additions were made over the years. "We adhered to the local custom of a white exterior with black shutters, which is in stark contrast to all the color and pattern in the interiors," says Schuyler.

ABOVE: A guest bedroom exhibits an air of patterned pageantry. "I knew that I wanted this guest room to have some drama, so I combined a remnant of discontinued chintz from a local shop with our Millerton stripe to create this cozy bed," Schuyler says. She scored the cornice boards at a Martha Stewart tag sale. "They were green, but I painted them red." A portrait of Jack, a beloved terrier mix who passed away, hangs to the side. It was a gift from Schuyler's parents.

A packed bookshelf in the "chatting room" is adorned with a multitude of favorite ceramics and collected finds from over the years. A mix of quirky Staffordshire dogs joins a ceramic cat, spill vases, a mercury glass vase, and local flea market items. The chairs are covered in the Stockton pattern by Flora Soames.

A neutrally-hued ceiling and a glimmery fixture in the dining area give breathing room to the short walls.

"This room was entirely white when we moved in, so I had to immediately tone it down." With the addition of color and pattern, the living room warmed up. The bookshelf color is Tate Olive by Benjamin Moore, backed by the same wallpaper surrounding the desk. Chairs were reupholstered, too. The sofa was renewed in a bright red linen. The armchairs were re-covered in a soft paisley print called Sanobar by Namay Samay.

LEFT: A burlap-shaded lamp from a small dealer in LA was one of the first gifts Schuyler received from her partner, Marc. It stands on a side table in the sitting room.

RIGHT: Blue serveware and dishes are stored in a dining room china cabinet.

OPPOSITE: In a corner, a desk purchased in Los Angeles provides a place to pen some thoughts. The wallpaper is from Jasper, a showroom by Michael Smith, Schuyler's former boss. The framed image of the dogs was part of the decor in Schuyler's first New York City apartment. The painting above the desk is from Schuyler's parents. Look closely: On the top corner hangs a little metal gunpowder flask.

ABOVE: A petite silver frame was gifted to Schuyler by a friend. "The photo is a shot of my father from World War Two," says Schuyler.

Upon Robert Kime wallpaper in a tiny room at the bottom of the back stairs that's jokingly referred to as the "Amuse-Bouche," Schuyler congregated pieces with deeper colors—greens, blacks, browns—into a vignette of framed prints, plates, and a pair of bracket wall shelves sourced at an antique store in Millerton, New York. She often has help growing her collection. "My brother Kyle combs flea markets on the weekends and texts me photos of things he thinks I would like. We are true partners in crime."

RIGHT: A handsome hallway features Aquarelle wallpaper, a new addition to Schuyler's collection. "Blue is one of those colors that works with everything. It's printed on a slightly textured ground, and resembles a hand-rendered watercolor stripe."

OPPOSITE: In the primary bedroom, an oversize Indian-style canopy bed from the 1930s hovers just below ceiling height. Here, Schuyler started with her Floriana wallpaper and curtain fabric. "That pattern is very bold, so the other fabrics had to take a back seat but still hold their own." Schuyler used Reverse Doshi Pop from her own line on the interior of the canopy. The leopard lampshade was purchased in Los Angeles. For subtle hits of color, a saffron floral quilt and a faded apricot pillow bedeck the bed.

LESSONS FOR A LAYERED HOME

STORE YOUR TREASURES FOR SOMEDAY. For this house, Schuyler wasn't going from a total blank slate where she had to buy all-new furniture. "I had things that I'd collected over the years, and then my parents died eighteen days apart. So suddenly, I had a ton of stuff that had belonged to them, and I was living in an apartment at the time with nowhere to put it." Schuyler knew that one day she would have the space to take advantage of all these amazing pieces. "I had five storage units. I had some in Washington, DC, and some in Los Angeles . . . and then during Covid, my boyfriend and I found this place and finally I had a space to use everything. So the evolution of the design really came from what I had."

IT'S OKAY TO NEVER BE DONE. Because Schuyler is always introducing new patterns, fabrics, and wallpapers, she's always playing around with re-covering items and switching things up. "My home's decor is always shifting. I've painted rooms three times. I've put wallpaper up and taken it down. It's my work, and it's also my passion."

EXPRESS YOURSELF ON THE OUTSIDE. Outdoor art, in the form of instructional botanical posters from the UK, turns a typical blank space in Schuyler's home into a fresh-air gallery. "I wanted something that made a huge impact but would also be easy to take in depending on the weather."

EMBRACE IMPERFECTION. Slight differences can have a big impact when collections come together. Schuyler discovered many of her mini Staffordshire pieces at flea markets. "One is missing his nose. I go for character versus perfection!"

DIVORCE DIM SPACES. Low ceilings in the dining room screamed for a touch of glam and glimmer, says Schuyler. "I got the mercury glass globe at the John Rosselli showroom in New York ages ago, and it followed me here from Los Angeles. It was the perfect thing to add a little sparkle."

OPPOSITE: A folkloric theme guided the design of this guest bedroom, enhanced by an overhead papier-mâché vine from Casa Gusto. "I wanted the vine to look like it was growing out of the corner," Schuyler explains. The coverlet was custom-made from an embroidered fragment she had saved. The wallpaper is the Millerton pattern from Schuyler's collection. "The stripes provide the perfect backdrop for the florals."

shopping with
JULIA COLLINS

COLLINS & GREEN ART
CHELSEA, LONDON

ARTFUL ABUNDANCE

One of the joys of social media is connecting with dealers from across the globe, which is how I first learned about Julia Collins's work and business. Her living room doubles as a gallery, and I enjoy seeing art hung in a home versus a showroom, especially in a space that's almost bursting at the seams. There's something magical about the ever-expanding inventory making its way onto the walls of the hallway and the entry, into bookcases, and even up the staircase. Art is everywhere, and it's all for sale; of course this is music to my ears. No room is off-limits when it comes to showcasing antique and vintage art, and there's the sense that things are constantly coming in and being sent out. Case in point: The cash wrap was piled high with orders ready to be packaged and shipped. Here, the joy of shopping is alive and well.

OPPOSITE: A shot of Beanie, Julia's little dog, captured from the studio. During the pandemic, Julia's studio was a holding space for desks for remote work. Now it's full of paintings. "I love being surrounded by beautiful paintings; I only ever buy things I love, so I am surrounded by beauty all the time."

FOLLOWING: "It's a typical Chelsea entrance," says Julia of the front door, which is painted in Chelsea blue (a nod to the local football club). "It will be bright emerald green next!" Surrounding the entrance is scented purple wisteria, which was gifted by Julia's mother when Julia and her husband moved in twenty-five years ago.

For Julia, art is not only a lens through which she views the world but also a place she returns to time and again. A compass and a foundation. And after working in finance for years, earning a master's in art history at Christie's, and taking time to be a full-time mommy, she has used this foundation as the basis for a whole new enterprise. In 2021, Julia launched her London-based business, Collins & Green Art, which combines her talent for accumulating art pieces with promoting its joys to others. It is a gallery, a showroom, a shopping destination, and a place of colorful, thought-provoking inspiration.

The surfaces are covered with frames full of florals and botanicals, seascapes, abstracts, and mid-century modern still lifes. There's something for everyone, and everything for someone. Customers often come seeking one thing and walk away with three more. Designers come calling to find a handful of pieces for a new project. The company is a must-visit for the art obsessed. But it's not all brick-and-mortar.

Julia says Instagram has opened so many doors. Indeed, the account is a scroll-addicting extension of the brand, enticing art lovers across the world with accessible price points. Where Julia finds and collects her art is her secret to keep, but she says that anyone can scout and build a collection by simply being aware in obvious places like flea markets, auctions, or online. Art exists everywhere you are, as long as you remember to look.

For Julia, this habit is innate. One of her earliest childhood memories is of taking a jaunt with her grandmother and proudly purchasing a teeny picture of a girl and a dog. The art is a beloved and sentimental highlight of her collection. Though change is constant, along with the rearrangement of framed art on her walls, it's never a problem. She always finds new pieces to fill in the blank spaces.

"I love being surrounded by beautiful paintings. I only ever buy things I love, so I am surrounded by beauty all the time."

Julia has one unbreakable rule about art: "If it moves you, makes your tummy tighten and your heart flutter, then you buy it."

Julia's English home features walls full of pictures that take various forms, from magazine pages and postcards to drawings by friends, prints, paintings, and even artwork by her children, who are now adults. If something "takes her eye," it is art, full stop, and it is displayed in a spot within the purview of daily living.

OPPOSITE: Julia recalls the effort she put into finding these just-right curtains for a favorite spot to sit and read. "When we moved into this house twenty-five years ago, we had a lot of work done and were running out of money by the time it got to curtains. These drapes in a basic and reasonably priced cream Indian cotton look very elegant, as they are thick and beautifully made."

LEFT: A busy intersection of art and books is the epitome of impermanence. "I swap out art all the time. If I sell something, it comes off the wall and I put something else up. The walls are constantly changing," Julia says.

RIGHT: A collection of nudes lines the stairwell all the way up to the bedrooms. "It's a bit of a family joke," Julia explains. "It wasn't deliberate, but it just sort of worked that way."

OVERLEAF: A kitchen wall swamped with treasured pieces is one of the most personalized walls in Julia's home. The bright collage at the top was done by Julia's daughter. Hidden behind the flowers is a painting by her son. The two paintings of children were gifted to Julia by her mother, who described them as "a girl and a boy like my twins." The pink and blue Matisse-style watercolor is by Julia's mother. "She had never drawn or painted, but when we all left home, she needed something to do and so took up painting; this is one of the first things she ever did and it is on the rescue list if there is a fire." The watercolor sketch above it, created by a close friend, depicts Julia's sixtieth birthday party in February 2020. "It was such a great evening, and little did we know what was about to hit the world! I feel very nostalgic about it."

at home with
COREY GRANT TIPPIN & CHRISTOPHER "TIPPER" STEVENS
BRIDGEPORT, CONNECTICUT

DARING DESIGNERS

Corey Grant Tippin and his husband, Christopher "Tipper" Stevens, have renovated a house in Bridgeport so that each room feels like its own little world with a distinct style and color palette. The spaces are thoroughly maximized—with lots of smaller rooms and a clever use of materials, from wooden wall cladding in a guest room to spotty Boussac wallpaper in the parlor. The kitchen is surprisingly spare, which makes the space more appropriate for contemplation and calm. The sink is in the butler's pantry, and the stove has been made to resemble a piece of furniture. Everywhere you look, story-filled mementos, personal photographs, and ephemera abound. There's a little guest room that is kind of daring with its bed on the diagonal and extra-large silk pillows. Much of the decor looks as if it's been collected over time—in fact, the lamps in the living room were found on the street, which is a fun story I can relate to.

OPPOSITE: A trio of framed photos offers a snapshot into Corey's past. Clockwise, from top: Andy Warhol's Union Square studio, The Factory, by Cecil Beaton (look closely—Corey is sitting on the windowsill in the background); Warhol superstars Donna Jordan and Jane Forth, by Bill Cunningham; and Douglas Hovey in drag, photographed by Billy Erb. The bust of Augustus, a plaster art student model, was found at a junk shop.

On the outside, the circa 1919 Craftsman bungalow home of Corey and Christopher presents as traditional, extremely charming, and, with its pairing of historic mossy and gold exterior colors, accurately sentimental. But step a few feet inside and the interiors are a plot twist, where other unexpected descriptions come to mind in what could feel like an endearing choose-your-own-adventure story.

Corey found the house in the late 1980s after he started working as a stylist for Martha Stewart. Before that, he spun in the close orbit of Andy Warhol, active in fashion and modeling in Paris and New York City. To make the house his own, Corey went thrifting, sourcing from junk shops and amassing affordable decorative space fillers. "Luckily, the house had not been disturbed," says Corey. "No one had really painted the woodwork. No one had messed up the early kitchen too much—there was no 1970s kitchen or any of that. It was kind of cute, so I just went with the nostalgic, sort of retro feeling it had."

Now the husbands dwell there together, along with Pansy, a smiley bull terrier who roosts upon the velvet daybed in the parlor to spy on neighbors in the mornings. A recently wrapped yearslong renovation managed by Christopher, an interior designer with keen know-how about all things architectural and mechanical, keeps the place comfortable and humming along. Despite additions of full baths and lots of behind-the-walls upgrades, "the bones of the house, the fundamentals, have stayed the same," says Christopher.

"Corey is the one who's touched every inch of this house," adds Christopher, whose subtle additions—furniture here, textiles there—elevate each space. Indeed, no area feels the same in personality or even color palette. Compare the parlor with its Pierre Frey Boussac leopard print—clad walls, the upstairs study turned cozy wood-sheathed bedroom that feels like a ship's cabin, and the sparse kitchen with its milky beadboard, green range, and hand-painted tile.

One thing that is consistent: cozy perches that hold the light, where Corey can often be found depending on the time of day. Christopher calls him "Mr. Outside Guy," and knows that if the weather isn't veering too chilly, he'll probably find Corey on the enclosed porch in the sun. "He follows the light, so he moves just as the sun moves through the house." In winter, as soon as four o'clock rolls around, Corey heads to the living room where the fireplace is, says Christopher. "We've got two sofas perpendicular to the fireplace, and you put your feet up on the end of the sofa, lie lengthwise, and just let the fire wash over you."

OPPOSITE: A lounge where Christopher and Corey rest and watch television features original woodwork and classic wallpaper in a Pierre Frey Boussac leopard print. A custom version of a Billy Baldwin St. Thomas daybed is outfitted in a red mohair velvet from Clarence House inspired by a fez hat on the nearby bust (see previous page). The mid-century chair and ottoman were discovered at a nearby antique mall and reupholstered in a tapestry print fabric from Dedar. Inside the pine cabinet, which belonged to Corey's mother, sit blown glass gazing balls created by a local artisan.

ABOVE: On the mantel is a "mishmash of things picked up along the way that felt good together," says Christopher. Upon the bamboo-style easel sits a plein air painting that's part of a bigger collection.

RIGHT: "Comfortable and cozy are the watchwords for this space," says Christopher. Here, a pair of Ralph Lauren sofas purchased from a former client were re-covered in a versatile and pet-friendly indoor-outdoor woven striped fabric. The fireplace is adorned with seashells collected from a nearby beach. The modern polished brass dome ceiling light is from Lawson-Fenning in LA, and flanking the fireplace is a pair of vintage Round Chairs by Hans Wegner.

OPPOSITE: This guest bedroom was designed for their friend Delia Doherty, an artist who visits in the summer. The bedding was inspired by a photograph of Andy Warhol lounging on the satin covers of a Victorian bed owned by Warhol's business manager, Fred Hughes. The paint colors in the room are by Farrow & Ball: Middleton Pink on the walls and Brassica on the ceiling.

"Having bedrooms of different designs makes it feel like they've evolved and acquired layers over time, and I like to think it's more European. It has a certain point of view."

ABOVE: The demilune table found at a local antique shop holds an assortment of Christopher's reproduction Greek vases as well as an oshiguma, a makeup face print, given to Corey by drag artist Tammie Brown. The Noguchi table lamp was inherited from Corey's friend Mae Alexander.

OPPOSITE: Here, the wall color is Churlish Green by Farrow & Ball. The bedspread was constructed from an Indian textile. In a nod to '70s decorating trends, the faux gilded wood lamps are staged on a pair of Lucite pedestals. The couple amasses busts for the living spaces. "More busts behind the bed because you can never have too many," says Christopher.

ABOVE: The custom oak and twine breakfast table in the kitchen can be seen from the butler's pantry. The paneled walls and the ceiling in the kitchen are painted in Strong White by Farrow & Ball.

RIGHT: A small collection of mismatched vintage tableware is kept in the glass-fronted cabinet.

OPPOSITE: "The kitchen came together by merging things we liked. Both of us love green, so the SMEG green range was a must," says Corey. Beloved hand-painted tiles from Mosaic House in New York add a patch of arresting contrast to the space. The original brass hood was designed by Christopher. Custom cabinetry painted in Strong White by Farrow & Ball is detailed with unlacquered brass hardware and classic soapstone. "It keeps things from being too cuckoo," says Christopher.

OPPOSITE: Hues from Picasso's classical period inspired the Moroccan zellige mosaic tile on the wall. The room is embellished with pink plaster on the walls, exposed beams, and handcrafted ceramic light fixtures. A dramatic staghorn fern hangs on a Gustavian-style corner cabinet that was found at a nearby antique center.

RIGHT: Christopher and Corey wrapped the former study in reclaimed wood and crafted matching shutters and a built-in bed. "The intent was to re-create Corey's childhood bedroom in a historic home in Essex, Connecticut, and give a nod to his obsession with Technicolor pirate movies from the 1940s and '50s. It's sort of a little ship's cabin," says Christopher.

LESSONS FOR A LAYERED HOME

TRY ALL YOUR FAVORITE LOOKS. Every bedroom in the house has its own character, says Corey. "It's a little bit extreme, but I like it."

DON'T HOLD ON TO ALL COLLECTIONS FOREVER. Corey admits to collecting many things over the years, but he's learned to dial it back, too. "I went through religious artifacts. That was an obsession for years. I went through taxidermy, another obsession for years. And then I was like, 'This is hideous. I'm going to get rid of all this.' And now I love good paintings. I really am attracted to figurative painting."

CREATE RICH COMPOSITIONS. When it looks very "one-note" in a house, it feels like a hotel, says Christopher. "Having bedrooms of different designs makes it feel like they've evolved and acquired layers over time, and I like to think it's more European. It has a certain point of view."

RELISH THE MIX OF THINGS AROUND YOU. When it comes to items in a house, it really is a process of accumulation, says Christopher. "Corey inherited a lot of things from his mother, who was an antique dealer, and he also picked things up on jobs over the years or at Goodwill or on the side of the road. I'm more of a collector. I care more about who the maker is. He doesn't care, which is also refreshing. It makes the home feel very comfortable."

REMEMBER, "MIGHT AS WELL" IS AN EXPENSIVE PHRASE. "I've discovered that when you begin a new project and you do one thing, suddenly everything else looks terrible," says Corey. "The work we did here wasn't a gut, but every room got reattended and reinvented."

OPPOSITE: For the bed, Christopher opted for a snake-themed statement pillow from Sean McNanney of Saved NY and a bedcover from Nickey Kehoe in Los Angeles. An intricately carved frame earns prime wall space above the bed.

AT EASE

LETTING GO

The most beautifully layered homes have an ease and grace to them, an effortless feeling that makes visitors feel comfortable and relaxed. I've learned that the key is in the eye of the beholder; it comes from the homeowners themselves, their personalities and attitudes about design, interiors, and entertaining. If your host is confident and comfortable in their home, you will be, too. Everyone included here embodies this casual, chic sensibility, and I believe it shows, not just in how each space reveals itself in the photographs but also how one actually feels there.

One common denominator is letting go. The moment we place too much value on something is the moment it dies. If our spaces are to feel vivacious and alive, our houses need to breathe. Things must come and things must go. Houses with souls allow for this process and always feel well used and well loved. An incomplete set of china on display might signify the time the party got a little too rowdy, or that vintage throw blanket may be covering up a paw print on the upholstery. An old wobbly dining chair might never be properly fixed and instead collect a stack of books. A new vintage piece of art might lean on a shelf for a few weeks before it's hung properly on the wall. Letting things go is so often the cure to life's ailments. We can't always sweat the small stuff when it comes to decorating; in the end, the whole point is to enjoy our homes and have fun, isn't it?

at home with
NATHAN TURNER & ERIC HUGHES
OJAI, CALIFORNIA

KNOWING YOUR SURROUNDINGS

D esigners Nathan Turner and Eric Hughes have merged their styles under a relaxed, Americana meets Californian ranch aesthetic. As consummate and pragmatic professionals, they picked a theme for their weekend cottage in Ojai and stuck to it. Editing what you live with is no easy task, but these two do it effortlessly. Composition, color, and materiality collide to create the most alluring vignettes throughout the home, from the flooring and wall materials to the perfectly un-styled coat rack by the front door. The home opens up to the outside throughout—this is California, after all—and the outdoor spaces receive the same consideration as inside, creating a relaxed, well-appointed place to entertain weekenders or laze around with the dogs.

OPPOSITE: An entry wall with hooks curbs the pell-mell of coming and going. It features hats and coats, a collection of art featuring the couple's Labradors, a mirror made by Nathan's dad for Nathan's seventh birthday, and Eric's keepsake handprint in a frame.

In 2017, a 1950s California cottage in Ojai caught the attention of designers Nathan and Eric. The home itself was modest, but the classic rectangular lot was nicely sized, and the outdoor spaces, although scrappy, had various fruit trees planted by a previous resident. It had been a ho-hum three-bedroom rental with a galley kitchen and interiors that lacked any meaningful updates. It was right in town, walkable to everything, and, say Nathan and Eric, an ideal property to be updated and flipped.

But about a third of the way through the process, their perspectives changed. "We started to build a community and spend time at the house, and all of a sudden we were like, 'Why are we flipping this? The house is great. We love it.' So we decided to make some different choices, really make it our own, and lovingly redo it," says Eric. That meant devoting more attention to additions like a new primary bedroom and bathroom and a second guest bathroom, and boosting the character of the rooms by introducing tactile, textural, and decorative layers to blend with their furniture and antique collections. Ultimately, when the construction was completed in January 2020, a jewel box had emerged, outfitted with cozy but deeply meaningful spaces in which the couple can gather, cook, rest, and recoup with friends and their two Labradors, Nacho and Wally.

When it came time to design the interiors, the home informed the couple's decisions. To begin, they resolved to draw from their personal inventory of cherished items they already owned, or pieces they had inherited or collected on buying trips to Europe or some of their favorite design events like Round Top in Texas or Scott Antique Markets in Atlanta.

"It was really fun for me to pull out a bunch of stuff that came from my family's ranch and items that I pilfered from my grandparents or that really fit that early California vibe," says Nathan. Absolutely everything on the walls is something personal to him and Eric. But the experience of filling the house was incredibly symbolic, too, says Nathan. "Especially at a time when we were nesting during the pandemic and had that time to pull out items and photos and frame them or reframe them and put some thought into it all." Eric concurs, "It was a really nice way to decorate the house."

"We both really knew what we wanted this house to be. We wanted it to have an old California feel to it."

OPPOSITE: On a side table in the dining room, high and low mix. Framed black-and-white Edward Curtis photographs create a scenic backdrop for books, sculpture, and a dusk-ready Coleman lantern.

RIGHT: In the dining room, vintage agave oil paintings lean on an industrial worktable found in Maine that is used as a console. The cast-iron bust of the Indian chief was found at Scott Antique Markets in Atlanta.

OPPOSITE: Vintage pressed-back dining chairs feature Ralph Lauren fabric on the cushions. The curtain fabric is also by Ralph Lauren. The antique Spanish iron chandelier is from Early California Antiques, and the nineteenth-century dining table was purchased in Belgium. The dalmatian statue, poised to greet visitors, is from an Hubert de Givenchy auction in Paris.

OVERLEAF: One guest room features Nathan's own citrus-packed pattern, dubbed "Orange Crush" and available at Wallshoppe. Upon it hangs a collection of art by Mary Maguire. Matouk linens bring a grid of green to the bed, and the headboard fabric is by Colefax and Fowler.

LEFT: A Nathan Turner Spencer sofa upholstered in lemony-toned Élitis fabric creates a sitting area within the bedroom. The rug is by Marc Phillips, and the curtain fabric is Ralph Lauren. The pair of vintage embossed Mexican Angel Pazmiño leather chairs was bought at auction.

RIGHT: Natural light and wisps of green are framed by a window in the handsome primary bath enveloped in tile by Ann Sacks and featuring lighting as well as fixtures and a tub from Rejuvenation.

OPPOSITE: In the primary bedroom, bold colors like Oakmoss by Sherwin-Williams upon the walls intersect with subtle textural and textile patterns. The antique lantern is from a Parisian flea market, and the antique trunk is from Wells, Maine. The Monterey Style bed is made by Art in Fine Forms in California. The bedside tables were found at Early California Antiques in Oxnard.

LEFT: In an homage to Julia Child, the kitchen features a pegboard wall for Nathan's cast-iron collection, which includes a mix of vintage and Staub cookware.

RIGHT: The breakfast room is home to a growing array of Mexican and Californian pottery.

OPPOSITE: Above the outdoor dining table hangs a vintage iron chandelier from Early California Antiques. The tablecloth is by Ralph Lauren. Nathan uses this space for projects, like making fresh compote using figs from the backyard tree, but also for outdoor dining. "We spend a lot of time outside. I love my outdoor kitchen. It was always something I knew I wanted to have, with a range and an oven. I love being able to cook out there."

RIGHT: On the outdoor kitchen table, a close-up of the cheery patterns donning a Mexican pottery collection. "We both love Mexico, and it's one of our favorite places to travel and explore. We started collecting these pieces at the beach in Malibu—we've now been collecting them for a long time. I love them as a display but as a functioning part of our kitchen, too," says Nathan.

FOLLOWING: In the backyard, a Modpools shipping container swimming pool was integrated into the landscape. "We enjoy it, but the dogs really enjoy it," says Eric.

LESSONS FOR A LAYERED HOME

YOU DO YOU. But together. At the end of the day, a shared appreciation for old California and personal histories helped Eric and Nathan land on a design direction early on. "It's funny with two decorators," says Nathan. "I think we both have our things that we enjoy more than the other. But we both really knew what we wanted this house to be. We wanted it to have an old California feel to it. We're both from California. We both understand what that is to each other. And so that part was easy. It was really about personalizing the house, and just leaning into making it not only look great but also be super cozy and comfortable and personal . . . I feel like we both contributed to that."

DEFINE THE LINE. Eric notes their differences: "Nathan likes a very layered look, and I like a cleaner look. So he would probably keep bringing more stuff in, and I would probably pare things back. But together we get to a happy medium that I think is a lovely result. It's not sterile, but it's also not overly chaotic on the other end of the spectrum. We find it's a nice balance."

ADD WHIMSY WHEN YOU CAN. Nathan's peppy citrus-themed wallpaper in the guest room is one clever way to weave in another California staple.

TEXTURIZE THE WALLS. The kitchen, like many rooms of the house, integrates board-and-batten, which brings a subtle texture to vertical surfaces. "We added the board-and-batten to give the interior a little bit of weight and that early California ranch-house vibe," says Eric.

FRAME THE LIGHT. A mirror is not always the answer! In the dining space, an antique diptych map of the United States, found at Scott Antique Markets in Atlanta, creates a reflective surface to bounce natural light into the room.

CELEBRATE FAMILY IN A BIG WAY. A gallery wall featuring various members of Nathan's family populates a wall in the living room. "My family, we have a ranch in Northern California that's been in my family for generations. And so that's my little ode to them and my California roots," says Nathan.

OPPOSITE: A mid-century desk in a shadowy living room corner hosts an oversize circa 1920 Swedish oil painting bought at an auction in Stockholm. The sofa fabric is Madeaux by Richard Smith, and the verdant ottoman is by Nathan Turner.

at home with
JESSICA STAMBAUGH
NASHVILLE, TENNESSEE

LOG HOUSE

I am always inspired to see creatives taking the path less traveled when it comes to decorating and living a life that rings true to their unique soul. It's not every day that you come across a log house, but Jessica Stambaugh happened to find this unique vernacular architecture and stayed true to form when renovating. There's an art to knowing what to keep and what to get rid of. Jessica resisted any urges to completely whitewash the living room and primary bedroom and instead honored the original wooden walls, chinking, and ceilings. Leaving the wood bare and not covering up the uneven logs that make up the wall structure feel almost radical.

Jessica's a lover of craft, folk art, and anything handmade, from wood-turned stools to colorful handblown glass.

OPPOSITE: Little spurts of color break up the dim caused by the surrounding wood and stone. Jessica created the blue-and-white footstool in the foreground during a wood-turning workshop.

On the center table, a distinctive hollow-core ceramic basket is just one of many handmade items in the home. Crafted by artist and educator James C. Watkins, it often holds plant clippings and handfuls of pretty things found outdoors. "I have filled it with moss to bring a bit of nature in," says Jessica. "I purchased it from a local craft school fundraiser; I was mesmerized by the technique and scale."

Tucked behind the front door, a Swedish bench re-covered in a blue-and-white Le Manach fabric lends a folk-art feel to the entryway.

loved this house, and everything had its own place," says Jessica.

The circa 1946 home, which had been owned by only one family, was in good condition, but Jessica immediately had ideas for the living spaces that hadn't been updated since the 1960s. "I thought, I'm going to be a steward of this house. It's a special antique that I get to preserve and put my mark on." She pulled up old carpeting and refinished the floors, and installed lighting fixtures to brighten dark corners. As in many old homes, the architecture posed restrictions. "The walls are immovable," says Jessica. "But in some ways, the limits help keep the design ideas more straightforward and simple."

Jessica painted paneling to lighten up different areas and then layered in color. The concrete chinking, which runs throughout the house, got touched up. In the kitchen, which was extremely dark and brown, she removed the cabinet doors and painted the cabinets inside and out for a more open feel. Drawing a floor plan helped create a structure for the place and establish spots for the bigger pieces of furniture. But to Jessica, styling the rooms is never a completed exercise, but one that's practiced regularly. "I update rooms in small ways, often monthly, by moving art around and rearranging small tables, pillows, and accessories. It helps me see the space with fresh eyes."

A few years in, Jessica has a domicile she fondly refers to as "spirited, warm, whimsical, and curious." Her touches of 1950s design and era-appropriate hues coalesce within spaces in ways that balance "the heavy weighted rustic interior with some ruched lampshades, skirts, and delicate details." The application of this aesthetic dovetails symbolically with her formative years and direction into design. "I once wrote a graduate thesis on American taste for folk art and modern-day nostalgia for rustic living, and it feels fitting to now be living in a house that reflects that story."

"Small spaces are powerful because they can be so immediately immersive."

Jessica had already been living in Nashville for three years, having made the move from New York in 2017, when her real estate agent called up one day and said, "You need to see this house." What the designer and avid craft enthusiast found was a well-loved yet timeworn capsule of a cabin that endearingly patches together elements of different eras. "When I was walking through, it had this grandmotherly energy to it. Someone

PREVIOUS, RIGHT: The handwoven blue striped carpet, purchased in Oaxaca, is layered with a shaggy and striped Tulu carpet from Etsy. On the coffee table, an embroidered woven throw from an antique mall contrasts with a tablecloth bought in India. The green curtain fabric, also from India, is floppy-top style. "This is basically a folded-over edge with a cord that creates the wavy loopy flap," explains Jessica. "I liked the undone whimsy of it."

OPPOSITE: Inside the dining room hutch, Jessica's collection of French painted plates is kept company by animals and the occasional vessel.

ABOVE: Mixed wood tones, mixed textures, and mixed mediums lead a point of view from the front room into the dining room. The long horizontals of concrete chinking here and throughout the house are painted in Old White masonry paint by Farrow & Ball.

ABOVE: Part passageway and mudroom, Jessica outfitted the floor of the enclosed porch in blue Mexican tile featuring a lively pinwheel pattern. "It has this optic element I like." In winter, the space safekeeps ferns and geraniums from frost.

OPPOSITE: Sometimes you need a whole hallway when a closet just won't do. To that end, Jessica has designated this as an all-inclusive zone for laundry and cleaning supplies, utility items, garden tools, tote bags, and straw bags. The orange broom in the rear and the multihued broom in the foreground came from the Tennessee Craft Fair.

OPPOSITE: While in the Hamptons, Jessica scooped up this vintage Murano flush mount fixture, which she had rewired for installation. "It's fanciful but with a little bit of restraint and clean lines to rein in the decorative whimsy. It features a feminine lightness and delicate elements. I'm naturally drawn to pieces from the '40s and '50s."

RIGHT: Using block prints sourced from India, Jessica created the Roman shade and the lampshade. The bright green metal nightstand was custom-made by a local metal shop based on an original design of Jessica's. "It wasn't originally intended for this room, but I liked how the green, blue, and pink all work with each other and play off the wooden walls." Bedding is a jumping-off point for other elements in the room. "It allows for more flexibility with changing up the accents around it," says Jessica.

FOLLOWING: An office corner organizationally sustained by IKEA cabinets holds remnants of formative creative experiences. "The framed document is a recommendation Loulou de la Falaise wrote for me following an internship in her studio between college and starting my career," says Jessica. "I sent copies to potential employers but had the original framed as a reminder of that wonderful experience. The chair in the foreground I designed and made with a local woodworker."

ABOVE LEFT: In an office corner, energetic patterns are in play. A chevron table skirt with bullion fringe enlivens the space while hiding a printer. A vibrant Schumacher wallpaper designed by Neisha Crosland hypes up the walls with its branch-laden motif.

ABOVE RIGHT: One of Jessica's strategies with paint—and color in general—is to balance dusty tones with bright, clear colors, or acid-like colors. Farrow & Ball's Old White is on the cabinets and walls, while the kitchen ceiling is in Moonraker by Sherwin-Williams, a pale acidic chartreuse. "Using that color here turns the needle away from quaint cabin toward fresh and unique and playful," Jessica explains. She layered peppy linoleum over the existing floor to brighten the area underfoot.

OVERLEAF: Cherished images convene where bedroom walls meet. The top center spongeware plate is from Jessica's paternal grandmother. The mid-century landscape painting is from the Brimfield Flea Market. The top left piece is a plein air watercolor Jessica made on a trip to a Tennessee state park. The squirrel drawing is from a local antique dealer.

LESSONS FOR A LAYERED HOME

DON'T FEEL LIMITED BY THE HOME'S ARCHITECTURE. While it is very cozy, Jessica's home isn't decorated like a typical log cabin with plaids and rusticity. "The extreme and restrictive style of the architecture hasn't restricted a very personal and pretty feel to the home," she says.

WARM UP TO A PROVEN FLOOR PLAN. Centering furnishings off and around a fireplace is often the best furniture plan, and it worked well in Jessica's living room space.

ACCEPT THAT EMPTY SPACES ARE PART OF THE PROCESS. Jessica says they allow for consideration. "Empty spaces don't need to be filled, and in that way I'm more of a modest maximalist in my personal style. I like to layer and then peel back, layer and then peel back."

OUTFIT YOUR HOME WHEN THE WEATHER CHANGES. This is especially impactful in the winter months, explains Jessica. "I like to add textile layers, like more rugs and throws."

GO BIG WHEN ROOMS ARE SMALL. A powder room is the perfect statement space, says Jessica. "Small spaces are powerful because they can be so immediately immersive."

OPPOSITE, TOP: Climbing the stairs is a band of hand-painted Hopi kachina dolls from Bahti Indian Arts in Santa Fe. Typically, they are carved from cottonwood.

OPPOSITE, BOTTOM: Strictly for personal projects, the pinboard in Jessica's home creative studio isn't just a place to unload possibilities. "I tend to keep pin boards—whether for personal or work—to be a real working space, and not overly composed."

at home with
GREG DOMRES & PETER NICHOLS
LITCHFIELD, CONNECTICUT

EASY BREEZY

Greg Domres and his husband, Peter Nichols (and their mini schnauzer, Bunny), live in a more recently built home that they've made into a charming, rustic farmhouse. It's situated a few minutes outside of town and sits on a large property surrounded by expansive meadows and mowed paths throughout. The home has the fastidiousness of a well-kept ship and the creativity of an artist's retreat—many objects are heirlooms from Peter's side of the family, and each room is chock-full of original art. There's a global feel but also a relaxed country-house-by-the-sea vibe. Greg has worked with top independent home retailers and seems to see his home through a visual merchandising lens. From a palette perspective, most of the home is painted an intentional white, and the colors in the original vintage art and assorted antiques really sing against this backdrop. The home has many open-plan spaces, but the couple makes them feel inviting and warm by carving out smaller seating areas and purposeful vignettes, particularly in the great room. A demilune table topped with ceramic mushrooms at one end of the space anchors the breakfast area, while two petite sofas floating and facing each other create a cozy hang-out space at the other end of the room. A guest bedroom and the dining room have decidedly darker palettes, moodier canvases that keep the home feeling balanced and true to both partners' tastes.

OPPOSITE: A collection of ginger jars, which exhibits the couple's love of blue and white, lines the top of the bookshelf.

"Comfortable and eclectic" is how Greg describes the composite style that outfits the Litchfield, Connecticut, home he shares with his husband, Peter. What's comfortable: the country house vibe, nature views that draw your gaze away from screens, and an ample number of chill-out spots. "We created moments throughout the house to pick up a book, take a nap, and hang out," says Peter. As for the eclectic, an array of original art engages you through the home, as do family heirlooms and robust collections of ceramics, textiles, and crafts. Greg, a design industry executive and an artist who creates bold textural fiber art using chenille stems, says the mix is about celebrating the objects between them but also leaving space for what's new. "If something resonated, we bought it, then figured out what to do with it," he says. This makes for a fun game for guests, says Peter, a design consultant. "Friends are always looking around to see what's changed."

The circa 1987 home with four bedrooms and 3,500 square feet of living area was in a very different state when they first stumbled upon it in 2007. But the ample space, light, and views of the property guided the home's evolution. An overgrown meadow featuring 4-foot-tall grasses and wildflowers is a "visual buffer to the outside world," says Greg. These days, it's shorn with a couple of simple walkways and is a living, interactive exhibit. "We added the paths to easily access the remote parts of the property," says Greg. "It's fun to walk out there when it's peak firefly season—the paths draw the eye and create this sense of mystery like you just have to know what's at the end."

"We created moments throughout the house to pick up a book, take a nap, and hang out."

ABOVE: This peculiar pack of charming and funky ceramic mushrooms is one of Greg's growing collections. "They are from a local artist, Souby, and came from Pergola in New Preston, Connecticut. It's an ongoing obsession!"

RIGHT: Small stacks of Wedgwood's simply elegant Edme china take up space on a few shelves. "Peter grew up using it as everyday china, so we added it to our registry when we got married and have been collecting pieces ever since," says Greg. "Some came from Peter's mom, and others we grabbed at various shops, including Privet House in Washington, Connecticut."

OPPOSITE: A narrow space called for this duly proportioned dining table from Montage Antiques in Millerton, New York. "We needed a slim one for the kitchen, and this was just right," says Peter. The rug underneath is a painted canvas from Black Point Mercantile, which Greg discovered at John Derian. It perfectly suits Peter's regard for the color blue. "It's my color that I go to. Every room is anchored by some kind of blue tone."

FOLLOWING: Peter and Greg worked with Kent Greenhouse in Kent, Connecticut, to install the stone slab steps. Seasonal "Open Days" garden tours and tips from head gardeners inspired the plantings. "Our style is eclectic cottage—lots of nepeta (catmint), and we've added layers from there," says Greg. "In the summer, it's all about bees, butterflies, and hummingbirds." "Heaven!" adds Peter.

OPPOSITE: The formal dining room is "best enjoyed on a winter night with a fire going," says Greg. The elevated fireplace, at table height, enhances the ambiance by bringing the glow up from the floor and out into the room.

ABOVE: "The antique silver candelabras were a wedding gift from Peter's mom, passed down from her own wedding, so they're not only beautiful but also have sentimental value," says Greg. The painting is by Timothy Wilson, a Maine-based artist. Greg's been collecting his work for years, and found this piece in Provincetown, Massachusetts.

LEFT: Dashing colors overlie the powder room featuring Cole & Son Geranium Rouge & Leaf Greens on Black wallpaper. "My grandmother used to have tons of potted red geraniums on her patio back in Kansas City," says Peter. "I wanted to bring that vibe into our house—this wallpaper felt like a perfect nod to her."

RIGHT: Sheared pathways guide walkers through an overgrown meadow to more remote parts of the property and afford special perspectives of the surrounding land.

OPPOSITE: A canopy bed that's been in Peter's family for generations is where he and his cousins slept during childhood summers. The headboard is upholstered in an Oscar de la Renta Home ikat fabric, paired with dark blue grasscloth wallpaper from Twenty2 in Litchfield, Connecticut. The red strié ceiling wallpaper is from Cole & Son, and the large vintage silk pillows are by John Robshaw.

All pillows and mattresses get vetted before visitors come to stay. "We make sure the pillows and mattresses are comfy for our guests. No lumpy, gross pillows here," says Greg. In the guest room, printed statement pillows by Antoinette Poisson are a darling final touch.

OPPOSITE: The kitchen's go-to spot for gatherings is a cushy sofa from Hammertown Barn cloaked in ticking fabric. It's also the perfect stage for pillows featuring Peter's needlepoint, a hobby he picked up during the pandemic. On the back wall, a vibrant abstract purchased at Christopher Filley Antiques in Kansas City invites bold pinks and yellows into the room's scheme.

RIGHT: An English oak dough bin found at an auction occupies a busy corner. The vintage brass lamp is from Greg's grandfather's jewelry store in upper Michigan.

LESSONS FOR A LAYERED HOME

AGE THE PLACE. For not-so-old houses, dress up the floors, says Peter. "Throw rugs are an easy and accessible way to add a bit of history."

OFFER CHOICES OF BASIC THINGS. Excess pillows in a guest room aren't overkill but a thoughtful touch, says Greg. "Eight pillows—some soft, some firm—present guests with options to tailor their own sleep experience."

GO BARE. Naked windows allow natural light to smother the loveseat where Peter likes to read and Bunny, the couple's mini schnauzer, keeps watch while they cook. It's a great reminder to let nature in!

CREATE STOPPING POINTS. The landing in Peter and Greg's house is an intentionally curated spot filled with books for guests to explore. "We added the chair to make it more than just a pass-through—now it's a cute place to pause and enjoy a quiet moment," says Peter.

USE WHAT YOU LOVE. "Everything in this house is about the dog and us," says Greg. "Nothing is considered too precious. We use the china and silver every day!"

OPPOSITE: Handmade plates from Greg's time running the decoupage studio at John Derian are tactile reminders of fun memories with John and the team. His favorite is the "eye bowl," which stares out into the room.

shopping with
AJIRI AKI
MADAME DE LA MAISON
PARIS

SETTING THE TABLE

There is no more classic Parisian apartment than Ajiri Aki's, on the top floor of a Haussmannian building in the heart of France's capital. A series of lined-up rooms opens onto a tiny wraparound terrace that makes for easy entertaining in this delightful home. The main living space features not a seating area but a large rustic wooden dining table that plays center stage for homework sessions, dinner parties, and casual gatherings with friends, which makes sense given Ajiri's hosting expertise. In this commanding space, glassware, linens, and platters are at the ready. The speakers seem to be always on, the windows are open, and the bookshelves are filled with equal parts books and personal ephemera. The apartment itself breathes in and out, and one can feel connected to something more: the history of the city and the gleeful nature of its inhabitants.

OPPOSITE: Ajiri's vast collection of tabletop goods affords her the opportunity to entertain, mix and match, or stage a photoshoot for her own entertainment. "I like having a variety so that I can play with different themes and moods every time I host." Here, stock of blue-and-white Burgenland by Villeroy & Boch, some nineteenth-century Wentworth plates, and some Lochs of Scotland plates.

To Ajiri, foraging in the brocantes or outdoor markets of Paris or around Provence and beyond is generally not about looking for something specific but about stumbling upon the unexpected and quirky treasure that can be used in at least five ways. It's a game to Ajiri, especially when others tag along to register what she's placed in her sturdy pull-wagon. But Ajiri has trained herself to trust her inner feelings about the things that enter her field of view. Scanning a dealer's table is an exercise in potential, where Ajiri can surmise the prospects for an unassuming container to hold seasonal buds (or other flora and vegetation), a petite silver tong to be an accessory for a buffet, or even a place card holder to become a quaint picture stand. "I've been doing this for so long, I can see all the possibilities."

Ajiri's brand, Madame de la Maison, dovetails inspiration and intentional joy through a sublime online collection of French antiques plus styling services meant to dress a table, or a room, with a sense of delight. Indeed, Ajiri is a cheerleader for the concept of *Gesamtkunstwerk*, a German term that roughly translates to "total work of art." It's meant to summarize how different creative forms conjoin to create a unified and cohesive entity.

Obtaining new objects, or arranging a lively tablescape, is often done in the spirit of togetherness, which has been a thread in the fabric of Ajiri's life, from her formative years attending weekly African Christian fellowship gatherings with other Nigerian families in Austin, Texas, to the regular socials she now conducts within her own living spaces for family and friends. A devotion to gathering is a cherished tradition, and one that prompts her to cast fresh eyes on her rooms time and again because it is where memories made with others remain. "I always say this: At the table, our souls flood. Our past and our present and our future are part of that table, whether you say anything or not, and there's something beautiful and special about being in communion with other people for the moment."

This desire to remain curious and refresh her surroundings is one that Ajiri brings to every spot around her home, as everything there has its own unique story that's constantly unfolding. "I love that I can look around my house and I have these stories." Indeed, her guests remind her how cozy they feel walking in the door. "These are the layers and layers of my life, and the years of experience, and the years of things that bring me meaning and joy. Everything here is something that was found along the way. I'm constantly adding to my collection."

"I've been doing this for so long, I can see all the possibilities."

PREVIOUS, LEFT: Ajiri discovered this nineteenth-century trumeau mirror at a fair in Chatou. It hangs in her salon/living room. "It needs to be restored so we can see the painting better, but I somehow enjoy the cracks and subdued color that tell a story of how old it is."

PREVIOUS, RIGHT: The scenic terrace is a source of enjoyment from spring through fall, and then some. "From the first warm day in March, I am on this terrace until the temperatures start to drop in mid-October, and even then I am out here with a big sweater on," says Ajiri.

LEFT: As a birthday gift for her daughter who loves to write, Ajiri found a typewriter with mint green keys. The illustration of Ajiri is by artist Jordan Betten of Lost Art. "He drew this when I visited his studio with the museum curator I worked for in 2006 after I had surgery for a tumor on my leg. It's a reminder that I am a survivor."

OPPOSITE, TOP: Etched windows on a cabinet lightly mask assorted glassware collected over the years. "I believe that using mismatched glasses ensures that guests won't mix their glasses up, but also I never get bored reaching in here to grab a glass and pour myself a drink. I never know what beautiful beveled, cut, etched, or faceted gem I will pull out."

OPPOSITE, BOTTOM: The "gathering magic" happens in the dining room, which is connected to Ajiri's salon/living room. "I approach my mantel like I would a merchandising window display, which is constantly rotating and arranging beautiful objects, candles, and flowers."

Ajiri found the table while on her way to meet a friend for dinner. "I turned down the wrong street and saw this table in the window of a woodworker who was closing his shop to retire." It was delivered the next day and has become essential to her lifestyle of bringing others together.

MANY THANKS

This book would not be possible without the remarkable individuals who have chosen to live creative, layered lives. Thank you for opening your doors, welcoming us so graciously, and showing us what it means to live fully in your homes. It has been incredibly moving, and we are thrilled to share your personal spaces and charming shops with the world, in order of appearance:

BUTTER WAKEFIELD
Butter Wakefield Garden Design Ltd
butterwakefield.co.uk
@butterwakefield

SEAN MCNANNEY & SINAN TUNCAY
Saved NY
saved-ny.com
@seanmcnanney
sinantuncay.com
@sinantuncay

ERIC GOUJOU
La Tuile à Loup
latuilealoup.com
@latuilealoup

AMBRICE MILLER
Relic Interiors
relicinteriors.com
@relic_interiors

JAMES COVIELLO
jamescoviello.com
@jamescoviellohome

ALICE MINNICH
Larger Cross
largercross.com
@largercross

GEORGIA TAPERT HOWE
georgiataperthowe.com
@georgiataperthowe

PATRICK "PADDY" O'DONNELL
farrow-ball.com/colour-consultancy
@paddy_od_1

INDIA HOLMES
Pelican House
pelican-house.com
@indiasallisholmes

KATE DONOVAN & LESLIE JOBLIN
Kate Donovan Studio
kate-donovan.com
@katedonovan_lifeandhome
@tupelo_honey_combover

SCHUYLER SAMPERTON
Schuyler Samperton Interior Design
samperton.com
@schuylersamperton

JULIA COLLINS
Collins & Green Art
collinsandgreenart.co.uk
@collinsandgreenart

**COREY GRANT TIPPIN
& CHRISTOPHER "TIPPER" STEVENS**
@coreygranttippin
Tipper Studio
tipper.studio
@tipper.studio

NATHAN TURNER & ERIC HUGHES
Nathan Turner Design
nathanturner.com
@nturnerdesign
Eric Hughes Design
erichughesdesign.com
@erichughesdesign

JESSICA STAMBAUGH
JS Interiors
js-interiors.com
@jessicastambaughinteriors

GREG DOMRES & PETER NICHOLS
thestemist.com
@gregdomres
@pdn_

AJIRI AKI
Madame de la Maison
madamedelamaison.com
@ajiriaki

MORE THANKS . . .

If you are reading this, then you have found your way to this last page of the last chapter. Thank you for the shared interest in celebrating our homes and living fully in them. Putting our homes together is an act of love through and through, and I feel so fortunate to have the part I get to play in this exercise of layering in my work and life in the home I share with my husband, Luis Illades.

I am deeply grateful to Christina Poletto, who has been a true thought partner from the very beginning—since that night so long ago when the idea for this book was born over many glasses of wine in a tiny Brooklyn restaurant. Your voice and thoughtful storytelling have elevated this book to another realm. Watching you connect with each subject was nothing short of masterful. Your passion for the written word has truly brought this project to life.

From the bottom of my heart, I would like to thank Manuel Rodriguez, who brought not only a brilliant, seasoned eye but also a sense of magic to every image in this book. Your dedication—your willingness to go the extra mile to "get the shot," as they say—was indispensable. There are few people with whom I could have traveled across the globe, collaborated so closely, and shared long drives and late nights talking about work, life, and everything in between. I could not have done this without you.

A heartfelt thank you to Angelin Adams, my editor at Clarkson Potter, who believed in me wholeheartedly from day one. Your trust and guidance have meant the world. Thank you for letting me share these beautiful spaces. And thank you to the rest of the Potter team, including assistant editor Darian Keels, art director Mia Johnson, production editor Abby Oladipo, and production manager Kim Tyner. Your deep industry knowledge and keen eye for quality have guided me and pushed me to produce something I am incredibly proud of.

To the friends, mentors, and colleagues in the design community who have supported me along the way: Thank you to Kate Berry, who first took a chance on me during my bookbinding days; Tori Mellott, who first showed me the editorial ropes; Anthony Santelli, who showed me how to style people and interiors as well as tell compelling stories; and to Stellene Volandes, Elisa Lipsky-Karasz, Michael Boodro, Sabine Rothman, Robert Rufino, Newell Turner, Carisha Swanson, Hannah Milman, Marcie McGoldrick, Elana Frankel, Sophie Donelson, Clint Smith, Dara Caponigro, Jessica Romm Perez, Anne Hardy, Christie Brown, Dayle Wood, Kathryn Given. I extend extra-special thanks to Elizabeth Blitzer, Molly Bates, and Christina Juarez for your unwavering and enduring support.

To my parents, Jack and Christine Reynaert: Thank you for always encouraging me to try new things and to dream big.

Creating a home is, at its core, an act of love. I feel incredibly fortunate to be able to blend my work and my life in the home I share with my husband, Luis—to whom I owe the most thanks. Your love and support mean everything to me.

INDEX

Afternoon color (Sherwin Williams), 164–165, 168
Ajax Diner, 174–175
Aki, Ajiri, 288–293
Angus, Peggy, 36
animals, 35, 38, 59–60, 98–99, 192
Anthropologie, 176–177
Antique Yellow color (Old Village), 97
antiques, 17, 38, 45, 47, 75, 85, 87, 92, 168, 239, 242, 250, 279
Aquarelle wallpaper, 202
Argul, Maite García, 176–177
arranging, 183
art, 69, 70, 75, 183, 207–213. *See also specific locations*
Art Crawl, 173
Art in Fine Forms, 242–243

Bahti Indian Arts, 268–269
Baldwin, Billy, 127, 216–217
banquette, 118–119
bargain hunting, 150
bathroom, 36–37, 95, 138–139, 226–227, 242, 280
Beaton, Cecil, 214–215
bedroom
　boldness in, 127
　calmness in, 36
　color for, 222–223, 242–243
　decor options for, 98–99, 122–123, 176–177
　fabrics in, 127
　furniture for, 127, 203, 242–243, 263, 280–281
　layering patterns and colors in, 150–151
　lighting for, 176–177, 242–243
　wallpaper for, 138, 140–141, 202–203, 280–281
　window treatments for, 122–123, 203
Bell, Vanessa, 178
benches, 32–33
Benin Bronzes, 70–71
Benjamin Moore, 85, 95, 97, 119–120, 194–195
Berber Stripe (Madeaux), 141
Betten, Jordan, 291–292
　& Company, 36
Biscuit color (Farrow & Ball), 132–133
Black Panther color (Benjamin Moore), 109
Black Point Mercantile, 274
black-and-white, 30
Bloomsbury Group, 178
blue color, as universal, 203
Blue Pot color (Farrell-Calhoun), 165, 169
boldness, 127
Bone White color (Benjamin Moore), 95, 97

book nook, 173
books, 140–141, 170, 186–187, 211
bookshelves, 24–25, 94, 98, 119–120, 133–134, 136–137, 176–177, 192, 198–199
Branca, Alessandra, 161
breakfast room, 244–245
brick, 80
Brier & Byrd, 119
bronze heads, 70–71
bunting, 162–163
busts, 222–223, 238–239

cabbageware, 104
cabinet, 46
camera, 98
candelabra, 112–113, 279
candle holders, 91–92
candlesticks, 175
Canford & Co Framers, 38
Canovas, Manuel, 26
Canton china, 103
Casa Gusto, 204–205
chairs, 38, 84–85, 122–123, 238–239. *See also specific locations*
chandelier, 72–73, 77, 128–129, 238–239, 246–247
Charlotte's Locks color (Farrow & Ball), 24–25
Chelsea entrance, 207–208
Chelsea Gray color (Benjamin Moore), 119–120
china, 35, 92–93, 141, 175, 196, 233, 259, 274
Chinese antique porcelain objects, 87, 92–93
chinoiserie sewing table, 84–85
Christopher Filley Antiques, 284–285
Churlish Green color (Farrow & Ball), 222–223
Clarence House, 216–217
Cocoon Home, 24, 36
Cole & Son, 280
Colefax, Sibyl, 141
Colefax and Fowler, 21, 128–129, 239–241
The Collected Garden, 104
collections
　of art, 69
　collaboration in, 201
　of color, 54
　as on display, 71
　handmade, 254–255, 286–287
　letting go of, 228, 233
　living with, 69–83
　narrowing down, 42

of old and new, 54
process of accumulation of, 228
record, 169
repurposing of, 57, 60
searching for, 42
storing, 204
tiny, 155
from traveling, 42, 54, 87, 92–93, 110, 173, 176, 247
unique discoveries of, 56–63
See also art; objects
Collins, Julia, 207–213
Collins & Green Art, 209
color
　boldness with, 144
　collection of, 54
　comfort zone of, 162
　comforting, 98
　confidence in, 19–40
　constraint by, 135
　contrasting, 144
　coziness and, 110
　definition from, 165
　embracing, 130
　flow of, 144
　multiple, 144
　from outside in, 21
　patterns and, 21, 24, 152–153, 162
　personalization of, 103
　principles for, 144
　on recessed window, 146–147
　subtle use of, 109
　variation of, 130
　See also specific colors; specific locations
conservatory, 30–31
console, 112–113, 135
Constantinou, Angela, 24, 36
container, importance of, 21, 24, 38
Cook, Ethan, 109
cookbooks, 174–175
corner space, 169–170
Coviello, James, 85–99
Coyuchi, 176–177
coziness, 178
Crown Point Sand color (Benjamin Moore), 95
Cunningham, Bill, 214–215
curiosity, 82, 93
Curtis, Edward, 236–237
cushions, 158
Cypress wallpaper (Howe), 141

David, Jacques-Louis, 141
demilune table, 223
desk, 169–170, 196–197, 250–252
dim spaces, 204

dining room, 76, 82–83, 84–85, 116, 131, 132–133, 193, 238–239, 278–279, 292–293
dining table, 19, 32–33, 84–85, 128–129, 155–156, 224, 274–275, 288–293
DNR Bricks cashmere throw blanket, 54–55
Doherty, Della, 220–222
Domres, Greg, 271–287
Donovan, Kate, 165–178
Dresser, Christopher, 41
Dulux 70GY 30/254, 155
Dutch door, 33

Early California Antiques, 238–239, 242–243, 246–247
East India (Waterhouse Wallhangings), 85
Élitis fabric, 242
empty surfaces/spaces, 132, 135, 268
entryway, 18, 20, 110–111, 234–235, 256
Erb, Billy, 214–215

fabrics
　in the bedroom, 127
　for blinds, 26–27
　for chairs, 122–123, 238–239
　for dining table, 82–83, 116–117
　for frames, 92
　for lampshades, 203
　repurposing of, 162
　on the wall, 178
　for window treatments, 203
　See also specific fabrics
The Factory (Beaton), 214–215
Falaise, Loulou de la, 264–265
family photos, 118–119
family room, 119
Farrell-Calhoun, 165, 169, 174–175
Farrow & Ball, 113, 130, 132–133, 138–139, 146–147, 161, 222–223, 259
fashion, interior design and, 85
fireplace, 94–95, 108–109, 268
floral pattern, 36
Floral Trail Wallpaper Original, 38
Floriana wallpaper, 203
flowers, 19, 38, 79, 104, 105, 116–117
folkloric theme, 204–205
Forth, Jane, 214–215
Fowler, John, 141
foyer, 164–165
frames, 75, 92, 199
Frank, Josef, 162
French folk art, 60
furniture
　for the bedroom, 127, 203, 242–243, 263, 280–281
　Danish armchairs, 109
　for living room, 109, 114–115, 168–169, 194–195, 218–219
　for the lounge, 216–217

gallery wall, 98, 158, 250
garden/gardening, 21, 38. *See also* plants
George Spencer Designs, 33

Geranium Rouge & Leaf Greens on Black wallpaper (Cole & Son), 280
girandole, 92
Gothic Cabinet Craft, 176–177
Goujou, Eric, 56–63
Graham, Salvesen, 38
Grant, Duncan, 178
green color, 21, 26
greenware box, 46–47
Grenney, Veere, 127
guest bedroom, 173, 191, 204–205, 220–222

haberdashery, 158–159
Hadley, Albert, 12, 101
hallway, 52, 74, 127, 203, 260–261
Hammertown Barn, 284–285
Hawkbury wallpaper (G P & J Baker), 138
Hicks, David, 127
Hidden Glade (Farrell-Calhoun), 174–175
Hockney, David, 168–169
Holmes, India, 147–163
home
　boldness in, 127
　cadence of, 127
　as canvas, 183
　cherished objects in, 71
　finding meaning in, 67
　as meant to be lived in, 71
　personalities in, 110
　progression of spaces in, 127
　stewardship of, 257
Home, Melodi, 135
Home Ikat fabric (de la Renta), 280–281
Hopper color (Little Greene), 20–21
Hovey, Douglas, 214–215
Howe, Georgia Tapert, 109–123
Hudson River School, 53, 98
Hughes, Eric, 235–250
Hughes, Fred, 220–222

imperfection, embracing, 204
inspiration, 42, 122, 162
Irving, Carolina, 122–123
ivy, 80

Jasper, 196–197
Joblin, Leslie, 165–178
John Derian, 274
Jordan, Donna, 214–215

Kane, James, 169
Kehoe, Nickey, 228–229
Kent Greenhouse, 274–275
Kime, Robert, 201
kitchen, 19, 50–51, 78–79, 88–89, 90–91, 118–119, 160–161, 224–225, 244, 284–285
Kögl, Hans, 128–129
Konig, Rita, 127

La Tuile à Loup ("The Wolf Tile"), 58–60, 62

lamps, 24–29, 35, 38–39, 46–47, 81, 86–87, 135, 146–147, 196, 223
lampshade, 19, 35, 54, 203
Lancaster, Nancy, 41, 129
Larger Cross, 102–103
Lawson-Fenning, 218
layered design
　as collected, 12
　constant changing of, 204
　curiosity in, 82, 93
　daring, 215–228
　details in, 17
　intensity and saturation in, 38
　lessons for, 38, 54, 82, 98, 122, 144, 162, 178, 204, 228, 250, 268, 286
　personalization of, 12, 250
　as storytelling, 54
　as visual language, 11
Le Manch fabric, 256
Lewis & Wood, 141
Liberti, Ron, 168–169
library, 24–25, 94. *See also* bookshelves
Lichen color (Farrow & Ball), 113
lighting, 38, 146–147, 242, 250, 286. *See also specific locations; specific types*
limestone technique, 103
living room
　color for, 40–41, 168–169, 194–195
　decor options for, 24–29, 43–47
　furniture for, 109, 114–115, 168–169, 194–195, 218–219, 250–252
Livingstone wallpaper (Colefax and Fowler), 128–129
Loftin, Taylor, 168–169
log house, 252–269
Loro Piana fabric, 114–115
lounge, 216–217
Lucite bases, 112–113

Madame de la Maison, 290
Madeaux, 141, 250–252
Maguire, Mary, 239–241
malachite, 149
mantel, 24, 103, 108–109, 218
Map Room, 80–81
Matouk linens, 239–241
McNanney, Sean, 41–55, 228–229
mentors, creative, 178
merchandising, 103
Mexican Angel Pazmiño, 242
Michals, Duane, 116
Miller, Ambrice, 69–83
Millerton stripe, 191, 204–205
Minnich, Alice, 101–107
mirrors, 18, 128–129
Morrison, Penny, 24, 33
Mountain Man toile fabric, 54–55
Mountain Meadow color (Farrell-Calhoun), 165
mudroom, 260
Muriel Brandolini fabric, 116–117

Nathan Turner Spencer sofa, 242, 250–252

INDEX 301

Nichols, Peter, 271–287
Night Vision color (Valspar), 75
nostalgia, 88, 93, 211–213
Oakmoss color (Sherwin Williams), 242–243
objects
    allure of, 103
    education regarding, 60, 88
    family, 50, 67, 98, 118–119, 250, 273
    flexibility of, 82
    for functionality, 38
    as holding story of time and place, 132, 135
    letting go of, 233
    love for, 17
    old and new, 21, 54
    research regarding, 60
    searching for, 24, 42
    staying power of, 150
    storing, 204
    success in finding, 17
    togetherness and, 290
    from traveling, 42
Ochre color (Benjamin Moore), 85
O'Donnell, Patrick "Paddy," 129–145
office, 264–265
Old Salem gray color (Benjamin Moore), 95
Old Village, 97
Old White masonry print (Farrow & Ball), 259
old world, 85–99
Oldwick, New Jersey, 101
open shelving, 158–159. *See also* bookshelves
Orange Crush pattern, 239–241
Orient Express, 42
Orleans Stripe wallpaper (Farrow & Ball), 138–139
Oro color, 184–185
outdoor space, 20–21, 22–23, 24, 38, 80, 155, 204, 246–247, 280
overthinking, 122, 162

paneling, 257
past, embracing, 98
patterns, 21, 24, 150, 152–153, 162, 185–205
Pelican House, 150, 162
Perez, Enoc, 113
personal taste, 41–55
personalization, 12, 67, 75, 110
Phair, Liz, 170
Philippe, Louis, 17
Phillips, Marc, 242
pinboard, 268–269
Pink Ground color (Farrow & Ball), 138
plants, 20–21, 22–23, 24, 80, 84, 104, 105, 110–111, 116, 226–227
Plateau color (Farrell-Calhoun), 165
platters, 57, 62–63
Plaza Hotel, 54–55
Pooky Lighting, 24
pottery, 56–63, 175, 244–245, 246–247
PPG, 40–41

prisms, 92
produce, as decor, 175
Pyne, Nancy, 101
Pyne Hollyhock fabric, 101

radiator cover, 18
Ralph Lauren, 218, 239, 242, 246–247
Raoul Textiles, 26
reading nook, 119–120
record collection, 169
refrigerator, 41, 50
Relic Interiors, 71
relics, 109
Renta, Oscar de la, 280–281
repurposing, 162
Restoration Hardware, 114
Reverse Doshi Pop, 203
Robshaw, John, 280–281
Rogers & Goffigon, 122–123
Royal Albert Hall, 71
rugs, 30, 41, 52, 54, 77, 162, 178, 186–187, 257, 259
Ruig, Rosi de, 24, 35

Sacks, Ann, 242
Samay, Namay, 194–195
Samperton, Schuyler, 185–205
Sanobar print (Namay Samay), 194–195
Saved NY, 42, 54–55
Schoolhouse, 176–177
Schumacher, 101
sculpture, 70–71, 75, 113. *See also* busts
Sea Serpent (Sherwin Williams), 176
seasons, 268
Setting Plaster (Farrow & Ball), 146–147
Shelburne Buff color (Benjamin Moore), 98–99
shelf display, 25, 35, 40, 52–53, 58–59, 61, 83, 104, 106–107. *See also* bookshelves
Sherwin-Williams, 164–165, 168, 176
sitting room, 72–73, 94–95
Sketched Stripe Green fabric, 32–33
Small Medallion wallpaper, 36
small spaces, 82, 122, 257, 268
Smith, George, 26
Smith, Michael, 196–197
Smith, Richard, 141, 250–252
Soames, Flora, 192
Şoray, Türkan, 53
Spode china, 92–93
St. Thomas daybed, 216–217
Staffordshire porcelain dogs, 35, 38, 98–99, 192
Stambaugh, Jessica, 252–269
Stevens, Christoper "Tipper," 215–228
Stiffkey Blue (Farrow & Ball), 161
Strong White paint (Farrow & Ball), 224
Studio & Store, 155
sunroom, 122
surroundings, finding meaning in, 67
symmetry, 85

tablespace, 82–83, 116–117, 149, 223, 288–293. *See also* dining table

Taconic Hills, 88–89
tapers, 175
Tapert Howe, Georgia, 109–123
Tate Olive color (Benjamin Moore), 194–195
Taylor Grocery, 174–175
tea sets, 175
terrace, 155, 291–292. *See also* outdoor space
terrines, 60
texture, 109, 250, 259
Thamutok, Pannawat, 168–169
Thonet, 84–85
Thornton, Izzy, 170
tile, 161, 224, 226–227, 242, 260
Tippin, Corey Grant, 215–228
togetherness, 290
Totten, Bill, 103
tradition, 93
traveling, collections from, 42, 54, 87, 92–93, 110, 173, 176, 247
Tree Poppy (Colefax and Fowler), 128–129
trompe l'oeil wall treatment, 103
Tulu carpet, 257, 259
Tuncay, Sinan, 41–55
Turner, Nathan, 127, 235–250
Turner's Yellow color (PPG), 40–41
Twenty2, 280–281

underpainting, 183
undertones, 144
unmatching, 82

Valspar, 75
vases, 78–79, 82
Vaughan Designs, 35
vintage, embracing, 98
Visual Comfort, 176–177

wainscoting, 95
Wakefield, Butter, 19–40
wall sconces, 36
wallpaper, 19, 87, 119, 128–129, 160–161, 202–203
Wallshoppe, 239–241
Warhol, Andy, 214–215, 220–222
Waterhouse Wallhangings, 85
Watkins, James C., 254–255
Wegner, Hans, 218
white paint, undertones of, 144
Whitfield, Robin, 169
Wilson, Timothy, 279
window treatments, 26–27, 122–123, 128–129, 141, 162, 191, 203, 210–211, 263
workspace, 88–89, 112–113, 169–170, 196–197, 250–252

Xuan paper, 150

First published in Great Britain in 2026 by Mitchell Beazley,
an imprint of Octopus Publishing Group Ltd
Carmelite House
50 Victoria Embankment
London
EC4Y 0DZ
www.octopusbooks.co.uk

An Hachette UK Company
www.hachette.co.uk

The authorized representative in the EEA is Hachette
Ireland, 8 Castlecourt Centre, Dublin 15, D15 XTP3, Ireland
(email: info@hbgi.ie)

Copyright © 2026 Benjamin Reynaert
Photographs copyright © 2026 Manuel Rodriguez

Published by arrangement with Clarkson Potter/Publishers,
an imprint of the Crown Publishing Group, a division of
Penguin Random House LLC
First published in the United States in 2026.

All rights reserved. No part of this book may be reproduced
or utilized in any form or by any means electronic or
mechanical, including photocopying, recording or by any
information storage and retrieval system, without the prior
written permission of the publisher. No part of this book
may be used or reproduced in any manner for the purpose of
training artificial intelligence technologies or systems. This
work is reserved from text and data mining (Article 4(3)
Directive (EU) 2019/790).

Benjamin Reynaert asserts the moral right to be identified as
the author of this work.

ISBN: 9781846016936
eISBN: 9781846016943

A CIP catalogue record for this book is available from the
British Library.

Printed and bound in China

10 9 8 7 6 5 4 3 2 1

Editor: Angelin Adams
Editorial assistant: Darian Keels
Designer: Mia Johnson
Production designer: Christina Self
Production editor: Abby Oladipo
Production: Kim Tyner
Compositors: Merri Ann Morrell, Hannah Hunt, and Zoe
Tokushige
Photography editor: Ugne. Pouwell
Copyeditor: Sibylle Kazeroid
Proofreaders: Robin Slutzky, Sigi Nacson, Andrea Peabbles,
and Nicole Ramirez
Indexer: Elise Hess
Publicist: Lauren Chung
Marketer: Allison Renzulli